Starting Advanced Mathematics

The Essential Foundation

Hugh Neill and Sarah Payne

CAMBRIDGE UNIVERSITY PRESS

CAMBRIDGE
UNIVERSITY PRESS

University Printing House, Cambridge CB2 8BS, United Kingdom

Cambridge University Press is part of the University of Cambridge.

It furthers the University's mission by disseminating knowledge in the pursuit of education, learning and research at the highest international levels of excellence.

www.cambridge.org
Information on this title: www.cambridge.org/9780521893565

First published 2002
8th printing 2012

A catalogue record for this publication is available from the British Library

ISBN 978-0-521-89356-5 Paperback

Contents

Introduction

This book is a revision and reference guide for students who have taken the GCSE/IGCSE mathematics examination, and who intend to go on to study for AS and A level mathematics, or for the International Baccalaureate.

In choosing the content of the book, the authors decided to cover those topics which were unlikely to be covered specifically in advanced textbooks.

Accordingly, the book is divided into three parts: the first, and largest, part consists of algebra (Chapters 1–12); the second deals with the sine and cosine formulae in trigonometry (Chapters 13–15); the third part is reference material (Chapters 16–18).

There are plenty of practice exercises throughout, and at the end of each chapter is a brief 'Test exercise' which enables students to assess themselves. Students who have previous experience with a topic should start by attempting the Test exercise. It gives the best idea of what is in the chapter, and those who manage it successfully could skip the chapter, and move on. However, the examples in the practice exercises in a chapter do address common pitfalls which are not always covered in the Test exercises.

Three essential items have been assumed in the treatment of algebra. These are: the product of two negative numbers is positive; the BODMAS convention; and the rules for the four operations for fractions in arithmetic.

The first trigonometry chapter revises right-angled triangle trigonometry, and subsequent chapters give work on the sine and cosine formulae.

The third part of the book makes no attempt to give practice exercises, but is intended to be available for reference when needed.

Numerical work is presented in a form intended to discourage approximation at too early a stage in the working. In ongoing calculations inexact numbers appear in decimal form like 3.456..., where the dots mean that the number is held in a calculator to more places than are given in the book. Numbers are not rounded at this stage; the full display could be, for example, 3.456 123 or 3.456 789. Final answers are then stated with some indication that they are approximate, for example '1.23 correct to 3 significant figures'.

The authors thank Cambridge University Press for their help and encouragement in producing the book.

1 Starting algebra

This chapter is a brief introduction to algebra. When you have completed it you should

- know what is meant by the words 'expression', 'terms', 'like terms' and 'unlike terms'
- be able to collect like terms and simplify expressions
- be able to work correctly with the numbers 0 and 1 in algebra.

1.1 Expressions

Suppose that there are 10 people at a party and 3 more people arrive. You will then have $10+3$ (or $3+10$) making 13 people at the party.

Similarly, instead of 3 more people, suppose another n people turn up (where n stands for an unknown number). You will then have $10+n$ (or $n+10$) people at the party.

These expressions, $10+n$ and $n+10$, are correct whatever the value of n. If you know the value of n, you can then calculate the total number of people. For example, if $n=3$, the total will be 13.

An expression like $n+10$ is an example of algebra, in which letters are used instead of numbers.

Example 1.1.1
Suppose that there are 5 people at a party, and that more people turn up. How many people will there be if the following numbers turn up?

(a) 17   (b) m (c) $n+10$ (d) $m+n$

    (a)   The total number is $5+17=22$.

    (b) $5+m$ (or $m+5$).

    (c) $5+n+10$, which you can write as $5+10+n=15+n$.

    (d) $5+m+n$.

Suppose now that you start with n people at a party, and they are joined by another n people. How many people are there altogether?

The answer is $n+n$, or you could say that this is '2 lots of n' and write $2\times n$.

In algebra the multiplication sign $\times$ is generally left out, and $2\times n$ is written as $2n$.

So $n+n=2n$.

Similarly $5 \times n = 5n$ and $3 \times 2 \times n = 3 \times 2n = 6 \times n = 6n$.

Always write $2 \times n$ *and* $n \times 2$ *as* $2n$ *rather than* $n2$.

Two special cases: the numbers 0 and 1

$1 \times n$ is always written simply as n.

Division by 1 leaves a number unchanged, so $n \div 1$ is just n.

$0 \times n$ is 0, as any number multiplied by 0 is 0.

Division by 0 is not allowed. Here is one of a number of reasons why.

Since $0 \times 2 = 0 \times 1$, division by 0 would lead to $2 = 1$, which is obviously wrong.

In fact, calculators give an error message if you try to divide any number by 0.

Example 1.1.2
Find simpler forms for each of the following expressions.

(a) $2 \times x$ (b) $5 + n + n$ (c) $2n + 6 + n$
(d) $5n - 3n$ (e) $2n + 3n - 5n$ (f) $3m + 2n + m - 5n$
(g) $3n + m - 2n$ (h) $2m + n + 3m$

    (a) $2 \times x = 2x$.

    (b) $5 + n + n = 5 + 2n$.

    (c) $2n + 6 + n = 3n + 6$.

    (d) $5n - 3n = 2n$.

    (e) $2n + 3n - 5n = 0n = 0$.   *The step* $0n$ *is usually left out.*

    (f) $3m + 2n + m - 5n = 4m - 3n$.   *Handle the* ms *and* ns *separately.*

    (g) $3n + m - 2n = 1n + m = n + m$.   *The step* $1n$ *is usually left out.*

    (h) $2m + n + 3m = 5m + n$.

1.2 Some language

Expressions
Each of the following is an example of an **expression**.

    $2n$ $5m + n$ $3n + 6$ $2x - 3y + 6$ 6

An expression can consist of a mixture of letters and numbers.

Remember that the letters stand for numbers. If there are two different letters they usually stand for different numbers.

Terms

In the expression $2x - 3y + 6$, the separate parts, $2x$, $-3y$ and $+6$ are called **terms**.

The expression $2p - 3q + 5r - 7$ has 4 terms.

$$2p \quad -3q \quad +5r \quad -7$$
$$\uparrow \qquad \uparrow \qquad \uparrow \qquad \uparrow$$

These are the four terms of $2p - 3q + 5r - 7$.

The expression $2n$ consists of just one term.

The expression 6 also has just one term.

Like terms

Terms in an expression which you can combine to make a single term are called **like terms**.

$2n + 3n = 5n$.

$2n$ and $3n$ are like terms, because you can combine them to make $5n$.

Collecting like terms

The process of combining like terms to make a single term is called **collecting like terms**.

$2n + 8 + 3n - 2 = 5n + 6$.

The like terms $2n$ and $3n$ make $5n$, and the like terms 8 and -2 make $+6$.

Unlike terms

Terms which are not like terms are called **unlike terms**.

$5 + 2n$

The terms 5 and $2n$ in the expression $5 + 2n$ are unlike terms.

$2m + n + 3m$

The terms $2m$ and $3m$ are like terms, but the term n is unlike both $2m$ and $3m$.

Simplify

The word **simplify** means 'find a simpler form for'.

$2m + n + 3m = 5m + n$.

The like terms $2m$ and $3m$ have been combined to give $5m$. The term n is unlike both the others and has to be left on its own. $2m + n + 3m$ simplifies to $5m + n$.

1.3　Simplifying expressions

In a college, if you have m classes each with n students, then the total number of students is $m \times n$. This is written as mn.

You can write the letters either way round, so $m \times n$ is either mn or nm. It is often helpful to write the letters in alphabetical order, for example in recognising like terms. This is not essential, but it is usually followed in this book.

This corresponds to the fact that it doesn't matter in which order you multiply two numbers. For example, $2 \times 6 = 6 \times 2$.

As special cases, $n \times n$ is written as n^2, read as 'n squared' rather than nn, and $n \times n \times n$ is written as n^3, read as 'n cubed'. The numbers ^{2} and ^{3} are called **indices** (singular **index**) or **powers** and are the subject of Chapter 6.

The expression $n^2 - 2n - 3$ consists of 3 unlike terms, n^2, $-2n$ and -3, and cannot be made any simpler.

Example 1.3.1

Simplify the following expressions.

(a) $2 \times 3 + 5 - 4 \times 2$　(b) $3x \times y$　　(c) $3x \times 2y$　　(d) $z \times z$
(e) $3k \times k$　　　　　　(f) $2 \times f + 3 \times f$　(g) $(-n) \times (-n)$　(h) $px \times qx^2$
(i) $2 \times x + 3x$　　　　(j) $(-2x) \times (-3y)$

(a) $2 \times 3 + 5 - 4 \times 2 = 6 + 5 - 8$ 　　　*Multiplication is carried out before*
　　　　　　　　$= 11.$ 　　　　　　　　　　*addition and subtraction.*

(b) $3x \times y = 3xy.$ 　　　　　　　　　　$3x \times y = 3 \times x \times y = 3xy.$

(c) $3x \times 2y = 6xy.$ 　　　　　　　　　$3x \times 2y = 3 \times x \times 2 \times y = 6xy.$

(d) $z \times z = z^2.$ 　　　　　　　　　　　*This is what z^2 means.*

(e) $3k \times k = 3k^2.$ 　　　　　　　　　$3k \times k = 3 \times k \times k = 3k^2.$

(f) $2 \times f + 3 \times f = 5f.$ 　　　　　　$2 \times f + 3 \times f = 2f + 3f = 5f.$

(g) $(-n) \times (-n) = +n^2.$ 　　　　　　*Remember that* $- \times - = +$.

(h) $px \times qx^2 = pqx^3.$ 　　　　　　$px \times qx^2 = p \times x \times q \times x \times x = pqx^3.$

(i) $2 \times x + 3x = 2x + 3x$ 　　　　　　*Multiplication is carried out before*
　　　　　　$= 5x.$ 　　　　　　　　　　　*addition and subtraction.*

(j) $(-2x) \times (-3y) = 6xy.$ 　　　　　　*Remember that* $- \times - = +$.

Don't forget that you must do multiplication before addition as in parts (a), (f) and (i) of Example 1.3.1. (Recall the BODMAS convention, Section 1.4.)

Exercise 1A

1 Put each of the following expressions into a simpler form.

 (a) $3-5+4$ (b) $b+b+7$ (c) $c+2c$

 (d) $3d+2d-12$ (e) $2e-7+5e+8$ (f) $4f+7-3f-7$

 (g) $6-g-4+g$ (h) $3h+4-h-3-2h-1$ (i) $4i+2i-7i+1$

 (j) $2\times g+5\times g$ (k) $3\times f-2\times f$ (l) $2\times x-3\times x+2\times x$

 (m) $4y-2\times y$ (n) $4z-2z-3$ (o) $2u-1-u\times u$

2 Simplify the following expressions.

 (a) $a+2b+3a+4b$ (b) $c-2d+2c-5d$

 (c) $x\times 2-3\times y-y+2x$ (d) $2x-y-y-y+4x+3y$

 (e) $2u-v+3w-u+v+w$ (f) $3l-2m+4l-3n$

3 Simplify the following.

 (a) $2x\times y+3x\times y$ (b) $2xy+4yx$

 (c) $ab+2b\times b-2ba+3ab$ (d) $2p\times 3p+4p^2$

 (e) $4q\times 4q$ (f) $3a\times 2b+b\times 2a$

4 Express the following in a simpler form.

 (a) $4g-2+g\times g-2g+4-2g$ (b) h^2+h+3h^2-2h

 (c) $2j^2-3j-6j+9$ (d) $2k^2+h^2-3h-2k^2+h$

 (e) $3l^2+11l+30-l^2+2l-9$ (f) $m^2-m-2-m^2+2m-1$

5 Simplify the following.

 (a) $p\times p\times p$ (b) $2q\times q\times q$ (c) $3r\times 2r\times r$

 (d) $2s^2\times s$ (e) $4t^2\times 3t$ (f) $2p\times 3p^2-4p^3$

 (g) $3\times x^2+2x\times x$ (h) $3\times 2y^2-4y\times y^2$ (i) $3z\times 4z^2-2z^2\times 6z$

6 Not all the following expressions can be simplified. Simplify those which can be simplified.

 (a) $4a-2a\times b$ (b) $4b\times a-2a\times b$ (c) $a+b+2ab$

 (d) $a^2-bab+2a^2b$ (e) $a^2-aab+2a^2b$ (f) $x^3-3xx^2+2x^2\times x$

1.4 Formulae

The area of a rectangle is given by

  $\text{area} = \text{length} \times \text{breadth}.$

When this is written as $A = lb$ it is called a **formula**.

You can find the area of a rectangle if you know its length and breadth.

In other words, if you know the values of l and b you can calculate the value of the area A by multiplying them together.

Example 1.4.1

In the formula $A = lb$, find the value of A when $l = 5$ and $b = 3$.

When $l = 5$ and $b = 3$, $A = 5 \times 3 = 15$.

Sometimes, there is a mixture of addition, subtraction, multiplication and division.

When this happens, you need to use the BODMAS convention: that is

B: Brackets must be simplified first
O: Order is next (**order** means the same as indices or powers)
D, M: Division and Multiplication come next
A, S: Addition and Subtraction are carried out last of all.

Some people use BIDMAS, where the I stands for Indices.

Example 1.4.2

A cardboard box, without a lid, has a square base of side b cm and a height of h cm. The area A cm^2 of cardboard required to make the box is given by the formula $A = b^2 + 4bh$. Find the area of cardboard when $b = 5$ and $h = 6$.

When $b = 5$ and $h = 6$,

$$A = 5 \times 5 + 4 \times 5 \times 6$$

Remember, multiplication before addition.

$$= 25 + 120$$

$$= 145.$$

The area of cardboard is 145 cm^2.

Example 1.4.3

The volume V cm^3 of a sphere of radius r cm is given by $V = \frac{4}{3}\pi r^3$. Calculate the volume of a sphere of radius 4 cm, giving your answer correct to 3 significant figures.

$$V = \frac{4}{3} \times 3.14159... \times 4^3$$

Calculate the 4^3 first.

$$= 268.08... \ .$$

The value of π is taken from the calculator, and is approximately 3.14159... .

The volume of the sphere is 268 cm^3, correct to 3 significant figures.

The three dots, ... , mean 'and so on'.

Example 1.4.4

Find the value of $a + 2a^2 + a^3$ when $a = 4$.

$$a + 2a^2 + a^3 = 4 + 2 \times 4 \times 4 + 4 \times 4 \times 4$$

Multiplication before addition.

$$= 4 + 32 + 64$$

Remember, in $2a^2$, only the a is squared.

$$= 100.$$

Example 1.4.5

Find the value of $2p \times 2p$ when $p = -3$.

Method 1

$$2p \times 2p = (-6) \times (-6)$$

Remember $- \times - = +$.

$$= 36.$$

Method 2

$$2p \times 2p = 4p^2$$

$$= 4 \times (-3) \times (-3)$$

Remember $- \times - = +$.

$$= 36.$$

Exercise 1B

1 If $a = 3$, $b = 5$, $c = 6$ and $d = 2$, find the values of the following expressions.

(a) $a + b$ (b) $b - c$ (c) $a - c - d$

(d) ab (e) $a + bc$ (f) $ad - bc$

(g) $a^2 - bd$ (h) $ad - c^2$ (i) $cd - b^2 - a^3$

(j) $a^2 + b^2 - c^2 - d^2$ (k) $ab + bc + cd - da$ (l) $a^3 - b^3 + c^3 - d^3$

2 If $x = -2$, $y = 3$ and $z = -4$, find the values of the following expressions.

(a) $x + y$ (b) $x - y + z$ (c) $4x - 3y + 2z$

(d) $-2x + y + 5z$ (e) xy (f) $2xz + yz$

(g) $yz + zx + xy$ (h) $x^2 + y^2$ (i) $y^2 - z^2$

(j) $x^2 - y^2 - 2xy$ (k) $x^3 + y^3 + z^3$ (l) $x^3 - y^3 + z^3$

1.5 Some important results to remember

Remember that:

$a + b$ means `add a and b'

ab means `multiply a and b'

$2a = a + a = 2 \times a$

$$(3x)^2 = 3x \times 3x = 3 \times x \times 3 \times x$$
$$= 9x^2$$

Don't forget that the 3 has to be
squared as well as the x.

$$(-3)^2 = (-3) \times (-3) = 9$$

Remember $- \times - = +$.

Test exercise 1

1 Simplify, where possible, the following expressions.

   (a) $a + b + c$ (b) $a + 2b - b + 2a$ (c) $x - 2z - y + 2z$

   (d) $2lm + l - m$ (e) $abc - b^2$ (f) $a \times b + c$

   (g) $a + b \times c$ (h) $2p \times p$ (i) $q \times 3q^2$

   (j) $pq \times 2pq$ (k) $4x \times 4x$ (l) $2xy \times 4xy^2$

2 If $x = 2$, $y = -3$ and $z = 4$ find the values of the following expressions.

   (a) $x + y$ (b) $x - 2z$ (c) $z - x + y$

   (d) $z - x - y$ (e) $2x - 3y - 4z$ (f) $x^2 + z^2$

   (g) $y^2 + z^2$ (h) $2xy$ (i) $2xy - yz$

   (j) $3z \times 3z$ (k) $2yz \times 8yz$ (l) $2xy \times 4xy^2$

3 A rectangular shaped room is to have wallpaper on the walls and ceiling. The length, breadth and height of the room are x metres, y metres and z metres respectively. The area A m^2 to be papered, neglecting doors and windows, is given by

     $A = xy + 2xz + 2yz$.

If $x = 4.6$, $y = 3.2$ and $z = 2.8$, calculate the area to be papered, giving your answer correct to the nearest square metre. (You will need a calculator.)

2 Brackets

This chapter shows you how to use brackets. When you have completed it you should

- know how to simplify expressions which contain brackets.

2.1 Brackets

Suppose that groups of 50 girls and 40 boys from each of 3 colleges meet. One way of finding the total number of students meeting is to say that each college provides $50+40$ students, and then multiply this total by 3.

You can write the total number of students as

$$3\times(50+40)$$

or, more usually, as

$$3(50+40).$$

The symbols '(' and ')' are called **brackets**, or parentheses or braces; when you see them, you generally start by working out the calculation inside the brackets first.

So $3(50+40)=3\times90$
$$=270.$$

Similarly $23-(26-22)=23-4=19$.

Example 2.1.1
Calculate (a) $3(5-2)-2(4-3)$, (b) $3(4(3-1)-(5-2))$, (c) $2\times(-3)^2$.

(a) $3(5-2)-2(4-3)=3\times3-2\times1$
$$=9-2$$
$$=7.$$

Remember BODMAS: brackets first, then multiplication before subtraction.

(b) $3(4(3-1)-(5-2))=3(4\times2-3)$
$$=3(8-3)$$
$$=3\times5$$
$$=15.$$

Work out the inner brackets first. Recall that $-(5-2)$ is the same as $-1(5-2)$.

(c) $2\times(-3)^2=2\times(-3)\times(-3)$
$$=2\times9$$
$$=18.$$

Remember that $-\times-=+$.

Exercise 2A

1 Calculate each of the following.

(a) $3+(5+2)$ (b) $4+(5-2)$ (c) $14-(5+2)$

(d) $9-(5-2)$ (e) $18+7(1+2)$ (f) $7(1+2)-2(4-2)$

2 Calculate the following.

(a) $5(2-4)+2(5-1)$ (b) $2(5+2)-4(3-9)$ (c) $4(2-6)-(3-5)$

(d) $2(2(6-2)-(3+1))$ (e) $-4(7-7)+2(6-8)$ (f) $5(3-12)-(5-8+3)$

3 Find the value of each of the following.

(a) $2(5+2(3-1))$ (b) $3(4-2(3-4))$

(c) $(7-3(5-3))$ (d) $-(2(4-7)+16)$

(e) $-((-3(1-4))-3(3-2))$ (f) $3(2(3-7)+9)$

4 Give the values of the following expressions in a form without brackets.

(a) $2\times(-2)$ (b) $(-3)\times(-4)$ (c) $(-2)^2$

(d) $-(3\times2^2)$ (e) $4\times(-1)^2$ (f) $-3\times(-2)^3$

2.2 Expanding brackets

So far so good. As the previous examples only involved numbers, you could always work out the expression inside the brackets.

But you can't always do the calculation inside the brackets. If there is a letter, which represents an unknown number, inside the brackets you need to look at it another way.

For example, in $2(n+4)$ you can't first add n to 4 and get a single answer.

The following four examples show you how to deal with cases like this.

$2(n+4)=2n+8$	①	$2(n-4)=2n-8$	②
$-2(n+4)=-2n-8$	③	$-2(n-4)=-2n+8$	④

Example ④, $-2(n-4)=-2n+8$, often leads to mistakes as it involves minus $\times$ minus = plus.

It is important to remember these rules.

plus $\times$ plus = plus	plus $\times$ minus = minus
minus $\times$ plus = minus	minus $\times$ minus = plus

Expanding brackets

Removing the brackets from an expression is called **expanding the brackets**, or sometimes **multiplying out** the brackets. You should know both these expressions, which will be used interchangeably from here on.

Example 2.2.1

Use the examples in the box on the opposite page to help you to expand the brackets in the following.

(a) $3(a-b)$ (b) $x(3+y)$ (c) $-2(3+x)$ (d) $-(2-x)$ (e) $-p(-x+y)$

(a) $3(a-b)=3a-3b$.   *This uses Example ②.*

(b) $x(3+y)=3x+xy$.   *Example ①, with $x\times 3=3x$.*

(c) $-2(3+x)=-6-2x$.   *This uses Example ③.*

(d) $-(2-x)=-1(2-x)$ *Example ④ , using `$-\times - = +$'.*
$\qquad\quad =-2+x$ *It is usual to omit the middle step.*
$\qquad\quad =x-2$.   *You could also write this answer as $x-2$.*

(e) $-p(-x+y)=px-py$.   *Example ④ again, using `$-\times - = +$'.*

The next example shows how you can expand brackets and then simplify.

Example 2.2.2

Expand the brackets in the following expressions and simplify as much as possible.

(a) $(3+x)+2(3-x)$ (b) $2(p+q)-2(p-q)$ (c) $(a+x)+2(a-x)$
(d) $a(p+q)-a(p-q)$

(a) $(3+x)+2(3-x)=3+x+6-2x$ *Recall that $(3+x)$ is the same as $1(3+x)$ which is $3+x$.*
$\qquad\qquad\qquad =9-x$.

(b) $2(p+q)-2(p-q)=2p+2q-2p+2q$
$\qquad\qquad\qquad\quad =4q$.

(c) $(a+x)+2(a-x)=a+x+2a-2x$ *This is the same as part (a), with a taking the place of 3.*
$\qquad\qquad\qquad =3a-x$.

(d) $a(p+q)-a(p-q)=ap+aq-ap+aq$ *This is the same as part (b), with a taking the place of 2.*
$\qquad\qquad\qquad\quad =2aq$.

$$\text{\textbf{Exercise 2B}}$$

1 Expand the brackets and simplify the following expressions.

(a) $2(x+3)$ (b) $4(y+2)$ (c) $3(2-z)$

(d) $5(t-3)$ (e) $4(3-2p)$ (f) $5(2p+3q)$

(g) $a(c+1)$ (h) $b(2d+3)$ (i) $c(p-2)$

(j) $d(h-5)$ (k) $m(m-2)$ (l) $n(3-n)$

(m) $2l(3-2m)$ (n) $3m(2m-4)$ (o) $2n(n^2-2n)$

2 Multiply out the brackets and simplify the following expressions.

(a) $-2(x+3)$ (b) $-4(y+2)$ (c) $-2(z-4)$

(d) $-3(2t-5)$ (e) $-a(2c-2)$ (f) $-2b(3-2a)$

(g) $-c(2c-d)$ (h) $-d(5-3d)$ (i) $-4l(3-2l)$

(j) $-an(4a-3n)$ (k) $-2n(3-2n-4n^2)$ (l) $-2m(3m-n+2n^2)$

3 Expand the brackets and simplify the following expressions if possible.

(a) $2a-2(a-b)$ (b) $2p-p(3-p)$ (c) $pq+q(p-q)$

(d) $xy-2x(3-y)$ (e) $2x^2-3x(1-x^2)$ (f) $2x(5+x)-3x(1-x^2)$

(g) $3ab-b(a+5)$ (h) $5x-2(x+3)$ (i) $a(2b-3c)+ac(7-2b)$

4 Multiply out the brackets and simplify the following expressions if possible.

(a) $x-(2x-3)$ (b) $a-(b+2)$ (c) $2a-(b-a)$

(d) $q+(p-q)$ (e) $4-(a-4)$ (f) $(x-1)-(x+1)$

(g) $a(b-c)+(ab+c)$ (h) $x(x+2)-(x^2-2)$ (i) $2(m-n)-(m+n)$

2.3 Multiple brackets

You could, if you wish, leave out this section on a first reading.

If you have multiple brackets, that is one set of brackets inside another, start by expanding the inner brackets.

Example 2.3.1

Expand the brackets and simplify $3(a-2(a+1))$.

$$3(a-2(a+1))=3(a-2a-2) \qquad \textit{Start by expanding the inner brackets.}$$
$$=3a-6a-6 \qquad \textit{Then expand the outer brackets.}$$
$$=-3a-6. \qquad \textit{Then simplify the result.}$$

You can sometimes simplify the result that you get when you multiply out the inner brackets. It is a good idea to do this if you can.

Here is the same example again.

Example 2.3.2

Expand the brackets and simplify $3(a-2(a+1))$.

$$3(a-2(a+1)) = 3(a-2a-2)$$ *Start by expanding the inner brackets.*

$$= 3(-a-2)$$ *Then combine any like terms.*

$$= -3a-6.$$ *Then expand the outer brackets.*

You get the same result both ways.

You often work with easier expressions if you simplify as you go.

Example 2.3.3

Expand the brackets and simplify $2\left(u\left(a^2-2ab\right)-u\left(a^2+2ab\right)\right)$.

$$2\left(u\left(a^2-2ab\right)-u\left(a^2+2ab\right)\right)$$

Start by multiplying out the inner brackets.

$$= 2\left(ua^2-2uab-ua^2-2uab\right)$$

$$= 2(-4uab)$$ *Then simplify the result.*

$$= -8uab.$$ *Then expand the outer brackets.*

Exercise 2C

1 Expand the brackets and simplify the following expressions.

(a) $2(3(1-a)+2(2+a))$

(b) $3((1-b)-(1+b))$

(c) $-(2(1-x)-(1-2x))$

(d) $-3(4(2+3y)-(5-3y))$

(e) $2(x(3-y)+3x(1+y))$

(f) $5(3x(1-2y)-6x(y+2))$

(g) $3(y(2-x)+x(y-2))$

(h) $4(x(z-3)-z(2x-1))$

(i) $p(2(a-b)+2(b-a))$

(j) $q(2(p-q)-3(q+p))$

(k) $x(-(a-b)+b(x+a))$

(l) $y(-2(x-y)+3(x+y))$

2 Expand the brackets and simplify the following expressions.

(a) $x(3(b-a)+2(b+a))$

(b) $3y(2(p+q)+2(p-q))$

(c) $x\left(2y(x+y)-x\left(y^2-y\right)\right)$

(d) $-3z(4x(2+3y)-2y(5+6x))$

(e) $2a(b(c-b-2)+3b(a-c))$

(f) $5(3x(1-2y)-6xy)-10x(2+y)$

(g) $3(y(2-x))-x+x(y-2)$

(h) $4(y(2+z)-y(1+2z))$

(i) $x(2x(y-z)+zy(x-y))$

(j) $2x\left(x^2-2x\right)-2x\left(2x-x^2\right)$

(k) $x^2(x-2(3-y))-x\left(x^2+2y\right)$

(l) $-m(2x+c(1-b))+x(mc-b)$

3 Expand the brackets and simplify the following expressions.

(a) $(4x)^2-(3x)^2$

(b) $(-3y)^2-3y^2$

(c) $4z^2-(-2z)^2$

(d) $4z^3-(-2z)^3$

2.4   Some important results to remember

The rules for expanding brackets like these are:

$$a(b+c)= ab+ac \qquad\qquad -a(b+c)=-ab-ac$$
$$a(b-c)= ab-ac \qquad\qquad -a(b-c)=-ab+ac.$$

The rules about signs are:

plus $\times$ plus $=$ plus   plus $\times$ minus $=$ minus

minus $\times$ plus $=$ minus   minus $\times$ minus $=$ plus.

Test exercise 2

1 Expand the brackets in each of the following expressions to get a single number.

(a) $3(2-5)$ (b) $2(4+1)$ (c) $5+(1-2)$

(d) $6-(1+3)$ (e) $6-(1-3)$ (f) $8-2(3-6)$

2 Expand the brackets in the following expressions and simplify, if possible.

(a) $a(a+b)+b(a+b)$ (b) $a(a-b)-b(a+b)$

(c) $z(z-3)+3(z-3)$ (d) $z(z-3(z+3))-z(z+3(z-3))$

(e) $(2x)^2+(-2x)^2$ (f) $(2x)^3+(-2x)^3$

3 Simple equations

So far, in algebra, you have been concerned with expressions, and finding simpler forms for them. In this chapter, you will move on to equations. When you have completed it you should

- be able to solve equations using systematic methods.

3.1 Equations

Suppose that $x + 2 = 3$ and you need to find x. Then you can see immediately that $x = 1$.

Similarly if $3x = 6$, you can see immediately that $x = 2$.

$x + 2 = 3$ and $3x = 6$ are examples of **equations**.

When you find the value of x which fits or **satisfies** the equation, you are said to be **solving** the equation. The value of x which satisfies the equation is called the **solution** of the equation.

The equations $x + 2 = 3$ and $3x = 6$ are both very simple, and you do not need to be systematic to solve them.

However, the equations $2x - 7 = -3x + 23$ and $2(3x - 7) = 4 - 3x$ are not so straightforward. It isn't easy to see their solutions by inspection.

This chapter will introduce you to systematic methods to solve such equations.

A formula, such as $A = lb$, is a special type of equation which is true for all values of l and b. In the equations above you are trying to find the particular values of x which satisfy them.

3.2 The balance model

It is useful to think of an equation as a balance.

For example, the equation $x + 2 = 3$ is illustrated in the diagram, with $x + 2$ in the left pan and 3 in the right pan.

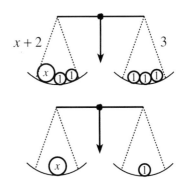

You can keep the scale pans balanced and solve the equation by removing two of the weights labelled 1 from each scale pan.

This illustrates the first rule about equations.

Rule 1

You can add or subtract equal quantities
from both sides of an equation.

Example 3.2.1
Solve the equations   (a) $x - 4 = 8$,   (b) $2x = 8 + x$,   (c) $7 = 6 + x$.

(a)	$x - 4 = 8$	*Add 4 to both sides.*
	$x - 4 + 4 = 8 + 4$	*Simplify both sides.*
	$x = 12.$	*The solution is $x = 12$.*
(b)	$2x = 8 + x$	*Subtract x from both sides.*
	$2x - x = 8 + x - x$	*Simplify both sides.*
	$x = 8.$	*The solution is $x = 8$.*
(c)	$7 = 6 + x$	*Subtract 6 from both sides.*
	$7 - 6 = 6 + x - 6$	*Simplify both sides.*
	$1 = x$	*Although the solution is $1 = x$, it is*
	$x = 1.$	*usual to write it in the form $x = 1$.*

In the last part, the equation is obviously solved, but it is useful to add a second
rule about equations. The rule is obviously valid.

Rule 2

You can swap the two sides of an equation.

The following examples use Rule 1 again, but the process of adding or subtracting
equal quantities from both sides of the equation has to be carried out twice.

Example 3.2.2
Solve the equations   (a) $3x - 4 = 2x + 5$,   (b) $5 - 3x = 3 - 4x$.

(a)	$3x - 4 = 2x + 5$	*Add 4 to both sides.*
	$3x - 4 + 4 = 2x + 5 + 4$	*Simplify both sides.*
	$3x = 2x + 9$	*Subtract $2x$ from both sides.*
	$3x - 2x = 2x + 9 - 2x$	*Simplify both sides.*
	$x = 9.$	*The solution is $x = 9$.*

(b) $5 - 3x = 3 - 4x$ *Add $4x$ to both sides.*

$5 - 3x + 4x = 3 - 4x + 4x$ *Simplify both sides.*

$5 + x = 3$ *Subtract 5 from both sides.*

$5 + x - 5 = 3 - 5$ *Simplify both sides.*

$x = -2.$ *The solution is $x = -2$.*

You could tackle these last two equations in other ways. For example in part (a) you could start by subtracting $2x$ from both sides; in part (b) you could start by subtracting 5 from both sides.

The point is that at each stage you choose a legal step which makes the equation simpler, aiming to get all the terms involving x on one side of the equation, and numbers on the other. If you can do that, you are getting somewhere.

You may find it helpful as you become confident to do some of the simplifying in your head, but take care not to introduce errors.

It is always worth checking your answer by seeing that it satisfies the original equation. So in Example 3.2.2(a), if $x = 9$, $3x - 4 = 23$ and $2x + 5 = 23$. It follows that $x = 9$ is correct.

Finally, here is a special case which is worth remembering.

Example 3.2.3
Solve the equation $6 - x = 7$.

$6 - x = 7$ *Subtract 6 from both sides.*

$6 - x - 6 = 7 - 6$ *Simplify both sides.*

$-x = 1.$

Notice however that the equation isn't solved, because x hasn't been found. You can remedy this by adding x to both sides, and subtracting 1 to get the following.

$-x = 1$ *Add x to both sides.*

$-x + x = 1 + x$ *Simplify both sides.*

$0 = 1 + x$ *Subtract 1 from both sides.*

$0 - 1 = 1 + x - 1$ *Simplify both sides.*

$-1 = x$ *Swap the sides. (Rule ②)*

$x = -1.$ *$x = -1$ is the solution.*

This seems rather long-winded. Just remember the rule for switching signs.

If $-x = a$ then $x = -a$, where a is any number.

Exercise 3A

1 Solve the following equations using the methods of this chapter. In each case check your answer mentally.

(a) $x + 3 = 5$ (b) $x - 7 = 6$ (c) $x - 4 = -3$ (d) $x + 7 = 2$

(e) $4 - x = 2$ (f) $7 = 2 + x$ (g) $5 = 4 - x$ (h) $2 = -x + 2$

(i) $3y = 2y + 2$ (j) $5 - 3z = -2z$ (k) $-2 + 2p = 3p$ (l) $3 + 3p = 2p$

2 Solve the following equations. Check your answers mentally.

(a) $2 + 3q = 2q + 4$ (b) $4 - t = 2 - 2t$ (c) $5 - 2z = 3 - z$

(d) $2 + 4y = 5 + 5y$ (e) $3z - 4 = 4z - 3$ (f) $x - 4 = 2x - 4$

(g) $2 - 4y = 3 - 5y$ (h) $7 + 2a = 3 + a$ (i) $4 - 3a = -4 - 4a$

3.3   The balance model again

To solve the equation $3x = 6$ it is useful once again to think about the balance model.

This balance model shows the equation $3x = 6$.

You can see that the left scale pan can be divided into 3 lots of x, and the right can be divided into 3 lots of 2, giving $x = 2$.

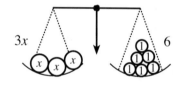

This illustrates the third rule about equations.

Rule 3

You can multiply or divide both sides of an equation by the same number.

Example 3.3.1

Solve the equations   (a) $7x = 21$,   (b) $-3x = 12$,   (c) $-x = 2$.

(a) $7x = 21$ *Divide both sides by 7.*

     $x = 3$.   *The solution is $x = 3$.*

(b) $-3x = 12$ *Divide both sides by -3.*

     $x = -4$.   *The solution is $x = -4$.*

(c) $-x = 2$ *Divide, or multiply, both sides by -1.*

     $x = -2$.   *The solution is $x = -2$.*

You may have noticed that part (c) deals with the awkward case in Example 3.2.3.

Dividing by -1 also shows that if $-x = a$ then $x = -a$, where a is any number.

You can also combine the methods of Sections 3.2 and 3.3 above. Example 3.3.2 illustrates this.

Example 3.3.2
Solve the equation $2x - 1 = 5x - 13$.

$2x - 1 = 5x - 13$	*Add 1 to both sides.*
$2x - 1 + 1 = 5x - 13 + 1$	*Simplify both sides.*
$2x = 5x - 12$	*Subtract 5x from both sides.*
$2x - 5x = 5x - 12 - 5x$	*Simplify both sides.*
$-3x = -12$	*Divide both sides by −3.*
$x = 4.$	*The solution is $x = 4$.*

You can also handle equations involving brackets by expanding any brackets first.

Example 3.3.3
Solve the equation $2(x - 1) = 3 - 4x - 5(10 - 3x)$.

$2(x - 1) = 3 - 4x - 5(10 - 3x)$	*Expand the brackets.*
$2x - 2 = 3 - 4x - 50 + 15x$	*Simplify both sides.*
$2x - 2 = -47 + 11x$	*Subtract 11x from both sides.*
$2x - 2 - 11x = -47 + 11x - 11x$	*Simplify both sides.*
$-9x - 2 = -47$	*Add 2 to both sides.*
$-9x - 2 + 2 = -47 + 2$	*Simplify both sides.*
$-9x = -45$	*Divide both sides by −9.*
$x = 5.$	*The solution is $x = 5$.*

You can check the solution.

If $x = 5$, the left side $= 2(5 - 1) = 2 \times 4 = 8$.
If $x = 5$, the right side $= 3 - 4 \times 5 - 5(10 - 3 \times 5) = 3 - 20 - 5(-5) = 3 - 20 + 25 = 8$.

Look at the solution carefully. It looks long and complicated, but it is mainly made up of the simple steps in Section 3.2. You need also to ensure that you handle the brackets correctly.

Exercise 3B

1   Solve the following equations.

(a) $2p = 10$ (b) $3q = 27$ (c) $5x = 20$ (d) $-3y = -15$

(e) $-2x = 14$ (f) $-3z = 0$ (g) $-6z = -72$ (h) $4k = 0$

2 Solve the following equations. Remember to check your solutions.

(a) $4x+3=x-12$ (b) $5b-32=2b-17$ (c) $3+2k=7+4k$

(d) $4-4k=-10+3k$ (e) $3m-14=5m+26$ (f) $m-12=6m+18$

(g) $2-3x=4x-12$ (h) $7-2n+3=4+4n$ (i) $2c+5-c=4+5c-19$

3 Solve each of the following equations, and check your answers.

(a) $3(a-2)=10+a$ (b) $2b-6=3(b-1)$

(c) $4(c-3)+2=c-10$ (d) $3(x-2)-x=5(x-3)$

(e) $k+2(k-1)=4-2(k-2)$ (f) $2(1-q)=3(2-5q)-4+q$

4 Find the solutions to the following equations.

(a) $x-(2x-3)=3x+11$ (b) $2a-(3+a)=a+(2a-3)$

(c) $5p-(4-p)=2p+8$ (d) $2(x+3)-4(5-x)=10$

(e) $7(b+2)+(8-b)=4b$ (f) $4-3q-(2-5q)=0$

3.4 Some important results to remember

The three rules for solving equations are:

> **Rule 1**
> You can add or subtract equal quantities from both sides of an equation.
>
> **Rule 2**
> You can swap the two sides of an equation.
>
> **Rule 3**
> You can multiply or divide both sides of an equation by the same number.

If there are brackets, you should multiply them out them first.

At any stage you may simplify either side of the equation, if this is possible.

Test exercise 3

1 Solve the following equations, checking that your answers are correct.

(a) $2-x=3$ (b) $4+2z=-10$ (c) $1-3z=15+4z$

(d) $2=4k-3+k$ (e) $-3u+2=2+u$ (f) $2v-7=2+v$

2 Find the solution of each of the following equations. In each case, check your answers.

(a) $2(w-3)=10$ (b) $5(x-1)=2(x+2)$

(c) $4-2y=3(1-y)$ (d) $4c+3(2-3c)=16$

(e) $5(2-t)=2(t-1)+4(t+3)$ (f) $2(h+1)-4(h-1)=-2+3(h-4)$

4 Fractions in arithmetic

You may not have noticed that in the previous chapter, all the solutions of the equations were whole numbers. In this chapter you will meet equations which do not have whole-number solutions. This is used as a way of introducing fractions. When you have completed the chapter you should

* be able to use fractions in arithmetic confidently.

4.1 Equations again

If you are solving the equation $2x = 1$, and attempt to divide both sides by 2, you get the solution $x = \frac{1}{2}$.

The number $\frac{1}{2}$ is called a **fraction**, and it arises from the attempt to solve the equation $2x = 1$.

Similarly the fraction $\frac{5}{6}$ comes from the equation $6y = 5$.

The fraction $\frac{7}{6}$ comes from the solution of $6z = 7$.

The fraction $\frac{a}{b}$, where a and b are whole numbers, comes from the equation $bx = a$.

Example 4.1.1
What is meant by the fractions   (a) $\frac{3}{5}$,   (b) $\frac{4}{3}$,   (c) $\frac{2}{1}$?

(a) $\frac{3}{5}$ is the number x which is the solution of the equation $5x = 3$.

This comes from the definition of a fraction (above).

(b) $\frac{4}{3}$ is the number y which is the solution of the equation $3y = 4$.

It doesn't matter which letter the equation uses.

(c) $\frac{2}{1}$ is the number z which is the solution of the equation $1z = 2$.

The solution of the equation $1z = 2$ can also be written as $z = 2$, so $\frac{2}{1} = 2$.

The fact that $\frac{2}{1} = 2$ means that 2 can be replaced by $\frac{2}{1}$ in fraction calculations, and vice versa. This is often useful.

Example 4.1.2
Solve the equations   (a) $4x = 3$,   (b) $-3y = 4$.

(a) $4x = 3$ *Divide both sides by* 4.

$\quad\quad x = \frac{3}{4}$.

(b) $-3y = 4$ *Divide both sides by* -3.

$\quad\quad y = \frac{4}{-3}$ *A positive number divided by a*
                                                     negative number is negative.
$\quad\quad = -\frac{4}{3}$.

In the last example, it is often better, especially in algebra, to leave the answer in the form $-\frac{4}{3}$ rather than the form $-1\frac{1}{3}$.

Exercise 4A

1 Find the solution to each of the following equations, expressing your answer as a fraction.

(a) $5x = 2$ (b) $2x = 7$ (c) $6y = 11$ (d) $4p = 5$

(e) $4x = 8$ (f) $3z = 12$ (g) $2n = 5$ (h) $7b = 5$

2 Write down equations without fractions which produce the following solutions.

(a) $x = \frac{1}{3}$ (b) $x = \frac{2}{9}$ (c) $p = \frac{8}{3}$ (d) $y = \frac{1}{5}$

(e) $a = \frac{2}{7}$ (f) $x = \frac{5}{1}$ (g) $b = \frac{1}{3}$ (h) $z = \frac{3}{2}$

4.2 Equivalent fractions

The equations $2x = 1$, $4x = 2$, $6x = 3$, and so on, all have the same solution because the equations can all be obtained from one another by multiplying or dividing both sides by the same number.

But the equations $2x = 1$, $4x = 2$, $6x = 3$, ... have solutions $\frac{1}{2}$, $\frac{2}{4}$, $\frac{3}{6}$, ...

So the solutions $\frac{1}{2}$, $\frac{2}{4}$, $\frac{3}{6}$, ... , must be equal.

Fractions such as $\frac{1}{2}$, $\frac{2}{4}$, $\frac{3}{6}$, ... , which are equal but have different forms, are said to be **equivalent**.

In this case, $\frac{1}{2}$ is the simplest of the equivalent fractions $\frac{1}{2}$, $\frac{2}{4}$, $\frac{3}{6}$, ... The form $\frac{1}{2}$ is said to be the fraction written in its **lowest terms**.

Writing a fraction in its lowest terms is called **cancelling**.

$$\frac{4}{8} = \frac{4\times1}{4\times2} = \frac{1}{2} \quad \text{or} \quad \frac{\cancel{4}^{\,1}}{\cancel{8}_{\,2}} = \frac{1}{2}$$

Cancelling is usually carried out by putting a line through the numbers being cancelled.

It is useful to have names for the top and bottom parts of fractions.

The number on the top is called the **numerator**; the number on the bottom is called the **denominator**; the line between is called the **fraction bar**.

Exercise 4B

1 Express each of the following fractions in its lowest terms.

(a) $\frac{9}{12}$ (b) $\frac{15}{12}$ (c) $\frac{4\times4}{4\times7}$ (d) $\frac{112}{12}$

(e) $\frac{24}{210}$ (f) $\frac{49}{56}$ (g) $\frac{128}{60}$ (h) $\frac{2\times7}{14\times5}$

(i) $\frac{3\times5}{3\times7}$ (j) $\frac{25\times6}{5\times9}$ (k) $\frac{4\times35}{6\times10}$ (l) $\frac{154}{220}$

2 Solve the following equations, expressing your answers as fractions in their lowest terms.

(a) $25x = 20$ (b) $6y = 8$ (c) $2a = 6$ (d) $12x = 15$

(e) $4b = 10$ (f) $26t = 65$ (g) $56x = 70$ (h) $6y = 81$

4.3 Rules for operations with fractions

The approach to fractions given in Section 4.1 enables the rules for the four operations for fractions to be derived. However, these rules are not derived or proved in this book, and are quoted without further comment.

4.4 Multiplying fractions

If you are trying to find $\frac{2}{3}\times\frac{3}{4}$, that is to multiply the fractions $\frac{2}{3}$ and $\frac{3}{4}$, you would use the following rule for multiplying fractions.

Multiplying fractions:

$$\frac{a}{b}\times\frac{c}{d} = \frac{a\times c}{b\times d} = \frac{ac}{bd}$$

For example, $\frac{2}{3}\times\frac{3}{4} = \frac{2\times3}{3\times4} = \frac{6}{12} = \frac{1}{2}$.

You can think of this rule as 'multiply the numerators and multiply the denominators'.

Example 4.4.1
Multiply the following pairs of fractions.

(a) $\frac{2}{3} \times \frac{4}{5}$ (b) $\frac{3}{7} \times \frac{5}{6}$ (c) $4 \times \frac{3}{8}$

(a) $\frac{2}{3} \times \frac{4}{5} = \frac{2 \times 4}{3 \times 5} = \frac{8}{15}$.

Multiply the numerators and the denominators.

(b) $\frac{3}{7} \times \frac{5}{6} = \frac{3 \times 5}{7 \times 6}$

$= \frac{15}{42}$

$= \frac{5}{14}$.

Multiply the numerators and the denominators.

Then you can cancel.

(c) $4 \times \frac{3}{8} = \frac{4}{1} \times \frac{3}{8}$

$= \frac{12}{8}$

$= \frac{3}{2}$.

From Example 4.1.1(c), you can write 4 as $\frac{4}{1}$, and then use the rule for multiplying fractions.

In part (b) above, you can cancel earlier. It usually saves time to do that.

Here is part (b) again, cancelling before multiplying.

Example 4.4.2
Find $\frac{3}{7} \times \frac{5}{6}$.

$\frac{3}{7} \times \frac{5}{6} = \frac{3 \times 5}{7 \times 6} = \frac{1 \times 5}{7 \times 2} = \frac{5}{14}$.

The factor 3 in the numerator divides into the 6 in the denominator.

4.5 Dividing fractions

Here is the division rule for fractions.

Dividing by a fraction:

$$\frac{a}{b} \div \frac{c}{d} = \frac{a}{b} \times \frac{d}{c} = \frac{ad}{bc}.$$

It is often remembered in words by saying, 'To divide by a fraction, turn it upside down and multiply'.

Example 4.5.1
Carry out the following divisions, leaving your answers in their lowest terms.

(a) $\frac{4}{7} \div \frac{3}{8}$ (b) $\frac{8}{9} \div \frac{2}{3}$ (c) $\frac{8}{9} \div 3$

(a) $\frac{4}{7} \div \frac{3}{8} = \frac{4}{7} \times \frac{8}{3} = \frac{32}{21}$.

Use the rule for dividing by a fraction.

(b) $\frac{8}{9} \div \frac{2}{3} = \frac{8}{9} \times \frac{3}{2}$

$= \frac{4}{3} \times \frac{1}{1} = \frac{4}{3}.$

Use the rule for dividing by a fraction.

Cancel before multiplying.

(c) $\frac{8}{9} \div 3 = \frac{8}{9} \div \frac{3}{1}.$

$= \frac{8}{9} \times \frac{1}{3}$

$= \frac{8}{27}.$

Recall that $3 = \frac{3}{1}$.

Then use the rule for dividing by a fraction.

Exercise 4C

1 Multiply the following fractions, leaving your answer in its lowest terms.

    (a) $\frac{3}{4} \times \frac{2}{5}$ (b) $\frac{3}{8} \times \frac{2}{3}$ (c) $\frac{1}{3} \times \frac{5}{6}$ (d) $\frac{4}{5} \times \frac{7}{12}$

    (e) $\frac{8}{9} \times \frac{3}{4}$ (f) $\frac{4}{5} \times \frac{15}{8}$ (g) $\frac{8}{9} \times 3$ (h) $4 \times \frac{5}{2}$

    (i) $\frac{2}{3} \times \frac{15}{8} \times \frac{4}{5}$ (j) $\frac{12}{7} \times \frac{3}{4} \times \frac{21}{9}$ (k) $\frac{2}{27} \times 6 \times \frac{3}{8}$ (l) $\frac{3}{8} \times 4 \times \frac{2}{3}$

2 Carry out the following divisions, leaving your answers in their lowest terms.

    (a) $\frac{3}{4} \div \frac{1}{2}$ (b) $\frac{3}{8} \div \frac{3}{4}$ (c) $\frac{4}{5} \div \frac{3}{8}$ (d) $\frac{1}{2} \div \frac{2}{3}$

    (e) $\frac{3}{5} \div \frac{4}{15}$ (f) $\frac{8}{5} \div \frac{4}{5}$ (g) $\frac{5}{24} \div \frac{15}{16}$ (h) $\frac{3}{8} \div \frac{3}{2}$

    (i) $4 \div \frac{3}{2}$ (j) $5 \div 8$ (k) $\frac{2}{3} \div 4$ (l) $1 \div \frac{2}{3}$

4.6 Adding and subtracting fractions

You probably remember that the rules for adding and subtracting fractions are more complicated than the rules for multiplying and dividing them.

Here are the rules for adding and subtracting fractions.

Adding fractions:

$$\frac{a}{b} + \frac{c}{d} = \frac{a \times d + c \times b}{bd} = \frac{ad + cb}{bd}$$

Subtracting fractions:

$$\frac{a}{b} - \frac{c}{d} = \frac{a \times d - c \times b}{bd} = \frac{ad - cb}{bd}$$

The process for addition and subtraction is usually written as in Example 4.6.1.

Example 4.6.1

Calculate   (a) $\frac{2}{5}+\frac{3}{4}$,   (b) $\frac{3}{7}-\frac{1}{3}$.

(a) $\frac{2}{5}+\frac{3}{4} = \frac{2\times4+3\times5}{5\times4}$

$= \frac{8+15}{20}$

$= \frac{23}{20}$.

(b) $\frac{3}{7}-\frac{1}{3} = \frac{3\times3-1\times7}{7\times3}$

$= \frac{9-7}{21}$

$= \frac{2}{21}$.

The two parts of Example 4.6.2 show cases in which the final result cancels.

Example 4.6.2

Calculate

(a) $\frac{2}{25}+\frac{3}{15}$,   (b) $\frac{5}{12}-\frac{1}{8}$,

giving your answers in their lowest terms.

(a) $\frac{2}{25}+\frac{3}{15} = \frac{2\times15+3\times25}{25\times15}$

$= \frac{30+75}{375}$

$= \frac{105}{375}$

$= \frac{7}{25}$.

(b) $\frac{5}{12}-\frac{1}{8} = \frac{5\times8-1\times12}{12\times8}$

$= \frac{40-12}{96}$

$= \frac{28}{96}$

$= \frac{7}{24}$.

If you are familiar with fractions, you may be thinking that you have previously used the lowest common multiple as the denominator (for example, 24 instead of 12×8 in part (b) above).

If you do this, then you may save yourself some cancelling at the end, but both methods will give the same result if you use them correctly.

You can also add or subtract fractions when there are two or more.

Example 4.6.3

Calculate $\frac{1}{2}+\frac{2}{3}-\frac{3}{5}$.

$$\frac{1}{2}+\frac{2}{3}-\frac{3}{5}=\frac{1\times(3\times5)+2\times(2\times5)-3\times(2\times3)}{2\times3\times5}$$

$$=\frac{15+20-18}{30}$$

$$=\frac{17}{30}.$$

The brackets have been added to make the process clearer.

You can leave the brackets out if you wish.

Exercise 4D

1 Carry out the following additions and subtractions, giving your answers as fractions in their lowest terms.

(a) $\frac{3}{8}-\frac{1}{5}$

(b) $\frac{5}{3}+\frac{1}{4}$

(c) $\frac{4}{9}+\frac{3}{4}$

(d) $\frac{4}{5}-\frac{1}{2}$

(e) $\frac{2}{3}+\frac{1}{7}$

(f) $\frac{11}{12}+\frac{1}{5}$

(g) $\frac{25}{8}-\frac{8}{9}$

(h) $\frac{7}{18}-\frac{5}{24}$

2 Carry out the following additions and subtractions, giving your answers as fractions in their lowest terms.

(a) $\frac{1}{2}-\frac{1}{3}+\frac{1}{5}$

(b) $\frac{1}{2}+\frac{1}{4}-\frac{1}{3}$

(c) $\frac{1}{2}-\frac{1}{4}-\frac{1}{5}$

(d) $\frac{1}{6}+\frac{1}{15}-\frac{1}{30}$

4.7 Some important results to remember

The **multiplication rule** for fractions is

$$\frac{a}{b}\times\frac{c}{d}=\frac{a\times c}{b\times d}=\frac{ac}{bd}.$$

The **division rule** for fractions is

$$\frac{a}{b}\div\frac{c}{d}=\frac{a}{b}\times\frac{d}{c}=\frac{ad}{bc}.$$

The **addition rule** for fractions is

$$\frac{a}{b}+\frac{c}{d}=\frac{a\times d+c\times b}{bd}=\frac{ad+cb}{bd}.$$

The **subtraction rule** for fractions is

$$\frac{a}{b}-\frac{c}{d}=\frac{a\times d-c\times b}{bd}=\frac{ad-cb}{bd}.$$

You should know how to cancel fractions and give the result as a fraction in its lowest terms.

Test exercise 4

1 Carry out the following multiplications and divisions, giving your answers as fractions in their lowest terms.

(a) $\frac{2}{3} \times \frac{5}{4}$ (b) $\frac{5}{6} \times \frac{2}{3}$ (c) $\frac{3}{7} \times \frac{14}{15}$ (d) $\frac{4}{7} \div \frac{3}{14}$

(e) $\frac{8}{9} \div \frac{16}{27}$ (f) $\frac{18}{35} \div \frac{15}{28}$ (g) $2 \times \frac{3}{4}$ (h) $1 \div \frac{3}{4}$

2 Carry out the following calculations, giving your answers as fractions in their lowest terms.

(a) $\frac{3}{5} + \frac{1}{2}$ (b) $\frac{3}{4} - \frac{4}{7}$ (c) $\frac{2}{3} + \frac{3}{4} + \frac{5}{6}$ (d) $\frac{2}{3} + \frac{3}{4} - \frac{5}{6}$

(e) $\frac{2}{5} + \frac{3}{4} - \frac{3}{10}$ (f) $\frac{8}{7} - \frac{3}{4} - \frac{1}{3}$ (g) $\frac{1}{2} + \frac{1}{4} - \frac{1}{8}$ (h) $\frac{1}{2} \times \frac{1}{4} - \frac{1}{8}$

5 Fractions in algebra

This chapter builds on the work of the previous one and introduces you to fractions in algebra. When you have completed the chapter you should

- be able to use fractions in algebra confidently.

5.1 The underlying principle

It is useful to remember that in algebra letters stand for numbers.

It follows that fractions in algebra work in the same way as fractions in arithmetic and follow the rules stated in Section 4.7, page 27.

In algebra, if you get stuck, it is often a good idea to ask yourself, 'If this were arithmetic, what would I do now?'

The answer will often tell you how to move on.

5.2 Writing fractions in algebra

Fractions like $\dfrac{x}{y}$ and $\dfrac{2}{y}$ are always written in those forms, but when the denominator is an ordinary number, not a letter, the fraction $\dfrac{y}{2}$ is often printed as $\dfrac{1}{2}y$, because it saves space.

Before tackling a problem involving a fraction like $\dfrac{1}{2}y$, change it to $\dfrac{y}{2}$.

5.3 Multiplying fractions

Use the rule 'multiply the numerators and multiply the denominators' as you would in arithmetic.

$$\frac{a}{b} \times \frac{c}{d} = \frac{a \times c}{b \times d} = \frac{ac}{bd}.$$

Just as in arithmetic, it doesn't matter whether you multiply first and then cancel, or cancel first and then multiply.

But usually it saves work to cancel first, and then multiply.

Example 5.3.1
Multiply the following fractions.

(a) $\dfrac{x}{y} \times \dfrac{y}{2}$ (b) $\dfrac{x}{y} \times \dfrac{y}{x^2}$ (c) $\dfrac{3pq^2}{r} \times \dfrac{r^2}{6pq}$ (d) $x \times \dfrac{2}{x^2}$ (e) $\tfrac{2}{3}y \times \dfrac{3x^2}{y}$

(a) $\dfrac{x}{y} \times \dfrac{y}{2} = \dfrac{x \times \cancel{y}}{\cancel{y} \times 2} = \dfrac{x}{2}.$

The two factors of y cancel.

The answer could be written as $\tfrac{1}{2}x$.

(b) $\dfrac{x}{y} \times \dfrac{y}{x^2} = \dfrac{\cancel{x}}{\cancel{y}} \times \dfrac{\cancel{y}}{\cancel{x} \times x} = \dfrac{1}{x}.$

The two factors of y cancel, and as $x^2 = x \times x$, the x on the top cancels with the x^2, leaving x.

(c) $\dfrac{3pq^2}{r} \times \dfrac{r^2}{6pq} = \dfrac{\cancel{3} \times \cancel{p} \times \cancel{q^2}^{q} \times \cancel{r^2}^{r}}{\cancel{r} \times \cancel{6} \times \cancel{p} \times \cancel{q}}_{2}$

$= \dfrac{qr}{2} = \tfrac{1}{2}qr.$

Notice how you deal with the numbers and all the letters independently.

(d) $x \times \dfrac{2}{x^2} = \dfrac{x}{1} \times \dfrac{2}{x^2} = \dfrac{\cancel{x} \times 2}{1 \times \cancel{x^2}}$

$= \dfrac{2}{x}.$

In arithmetic, 2 can be written as $\tfrac{2}{1}$. This is the same in algebra, so write x as $\dfrac{x}{1}$.

(e) $\tfrac{2}{3}y \times \dfrac{3x^2}{y} = \dfrac{2y}{3} \times \dfrac{3x^2}{y}$

$= \dfrac{2 \times \cancel{y} \times \cancel{3} \times x^2}{\cancel{3} \times \cancel{y}}$

$= \dfrac{2x^2}{1} = 2x^2.$

Write $\tfrac{2}{3}y$ as $\dfrac{2y}{3}$.

Recall that $\dfrac{x^2}{1}$ is the same as x^2.

Exercise 5A

1 Carry out each of the following multiplications.

(a) $\dfrac{x}{2z} \times \dfrac{3y}{x}$ (b) $\tfrac{1}{2}p \times \dfrac{q}{p}$ (c) $\dfrac{4x}{3} \times \dfrac{y}{2x}$ (d) $\dfrac{pq}{r} \times \dfrac{pr}{q}$

(e) $\dfrac{a}{bc} \times \dfrac{b}{ac}$ (f) $\dfrac{mn}{2p} \times \dfrac{np}{m}$ (g) $\dfrac{4x}{3y} \times \dfrac{6xy}{5}$ (h) $\tfrac{1}{3}b \times \dfrac{a}{2b}$

2 Simplify the following fractions.

(a) $\dfrac{a^2}{b} \times \dfrac{b^3}{a}$ (b) $\dfrac{x^2}{yz} \times \dfrac{y^3}{xz}$ (c) $\dfrac{pq}{r^3} \times \dfrac{pr}{q^3}$ (d) $\dfrac{xy^2}{x^3} \times \dfrac{x^2}{y^3}$

(e) $\dfrac{q^3}{r^2} \times \dfrac{p}{q^2} \times \dfrac{q}{p}$ (f) $\dfrac{x^2y}{z^2} \times \dfrac{yz^2}{x^3}$ (g) $\dfrac{a}{b} \times \dfrac{b}{c} \times \dfrac{c}{a}$ (h) $\dfrac{nx}{my} \times \dfrac{m^2y^2}{nx^2}$

3 Multiply each of the following.

(a) $\dfrac{x}{2y^2} \times \dfrac{1}{2}x$ (b) $\dfrac{2lmn}{3m^2} \times \dfrac{6m}{ln^2}$ (c) $\dfrac{3}{x^2} \times \dfrac{1}{9}x \times \dfrac{xy^2}{3x^2}$ (d) $2 \times \dfrac{1}{3}xy \times \dfrac{x}{y^2}$

(e) $\dfrac{3x^2}{4y} \times \dfrac{y^2}{6x}$ (f) $\dfrac{2pq^3}{5q} \times \dfrac{15}{3pq}$ (g) $\dfrac{2}{5}x^3 \times \dfrac{y}{4x}$ (h) $\dfrac{14a^2}{4ab^2} \times \dfrac{3ab^3}{7b}$

5.4 Dividing fractions

The rule is the same as for arithmetic.

$$\frac{a}{b} \div \frac{c}{d} = \frac{a}{b} \times \frac{d}{c} = \frac{ad}{bc}.$$

Example 5.4.1

Carry out the following divisions.

(a) $\dfrac{x}{y} \div \dfrac{1}{x}$ (b) $\dfrac{p}{3q} \div \dfrac{p^2}{6q^3}$ (c) $\dfrac{6s}{t^2} \div 2t$

(a) $\dfrac{x}{y} \div \dfrac{1}{x} = \dfrac{x}{y} \times \dfrac{x}{1} = \dfrac{x \times x}{y \times 1}$

$= \dfrac{x^2}{y}.$

The 'turn the second fraction upside down and multiply' rule has been used.
No cancelling is possible.

(b) $\dfrac{p}{3q} \div \dfrac{p^2}{6q^3} = \dfrac{p}{3q} \times \dfrac{6q^3}{p^2}$

$= \dfrac{\cancel{p}}{\cancel{3q}} \times \dfrac{\cancel{6}^2 \cancel{q^3} q^2}{\cancel{p^2} p}$

$= \dfrac{2q^2}{p}.$

Notice how you deal with the numbers and all the letters independently.

(c) $\dfrac{6s}{t^2} \div 2t = \dfrac{6s}{t^2} \div \dfrac{2t}{1}$

As $2t$ is the same as $\dfrac{2t}{1}$, dividing by

$= \dfrac{6s}{t^2} \times \dfrac{1}{2t} = \dfrac{\overset{3}{\cancel{6}} \times s \times 1}{t^2 \times \cancel{2} \times t}$

$2t$ is the same as multiplying by $\dfrac{1}{2t}$.

$= \dfrac{3s}{t^3}.$

Exercise 5B

1 Express each of the following fractions in its lowest terms.

(a) $\dfrac{x}{y} \div \dfrac{1}{y}$ (b) $\dfrac{a^2}{b^2} \div \dfrac{a}{b}$ (c) $\dfrac{p^2}{q^2} \div \dfrac{p^2}{q}$ (d) $\dfrac{c^3}{d} \div \dfrac{c^2}{d^2}$

(e) $\dfrac{p}{qr} \div \dfrac{q}{pr}$ (f) $\dfrac{2x^2}{y} \div \dfrac{x}{6}$ (g) $\dfrac{5xy^2}{2y} \div \dfrac{10x}{y}$ (h) $\dfrac{3u^2}{2v} \div \dfrac{5u}{4v^2}$

2 Carry out the following divisions giving your answers in their lowest terms.

(a) $\dfrac{3c}{d} \div c$ (b) $h \div \dfrac{k^2}{2h^2}$ (c) $\tfrac{1}{2} l^3 \div l$ (d) $\tfrac{1}{3} pq^2 \div \tfrac{1}{2} pq$

(e) $\tfrac{2}{3} a \div \tfrac{3}{4} ab$ (f) $\tfrac{3}{5} uv^2 \div \tfrac{3}{10} u^2 v$ (g) $\tfrac{1}{4} x^3 \div 6x^2$ (h) $\tfrac{3}{7} pq \div \tfrac{3}{14} q$

5.5 Adding and subtracting fractions

The rules are the same as for arithmetic, $\dfrac{a}{b} + \dfrac{c}{d} = \dfrac{ad+cb}{bd}$ and $\dfrac{a}{b} - \dfrac{c}{d} = \dfrac{ad-cb}{bd}$.

Example 5.5.1

Calculate   (a) $\dfrac{x}{2} + \dfrac{x}{3}$,   (b) $\tfrac{1}{2} x + \tfrac{1}{3} x$,   (c) $\dfrac{x}{3} - \dfrac{y}{4}$,   (d) $\dfrac{3}{x} + \dfrac{4}{x}$,

(e) $\dfrac{3}{x} + \dfrac{4}{y}$,   (f) $2x - \dfrac{5}{y}$.

(a) $\dfrac{x}{2} + \dfrac{x}{3} = \dfrac{x \times 3 + x \times 2}{6}$

The denominator is $2 \times 3 = 6$.

$= \dfrac{3x + 2x}{6} = \dfrac{5x}{6}.$

$3x$ and $2x$ are like terms, so they are added to give $5x$.

$\dfrac{5x}{6}$ may be printed as $\tfrac{5}{6} x$.

(b) $\tfrac{1}{2} x + \tfrac{1}{3} x = \dfrac{x}{2} + \dfrac{x}{3} = \dfrac{5x}{6}.$

This is the same as part (a).

(c) $\dfrac{x}{3} - \dfrac{y}{4} = \dfrac{x \times 4 - y \times 3}{12}$

$\qquad = \dfrac{4x - 3y}{12}.$

4x and 3y are unlike terms, so this cannot be simplified further.

(d) $\dfrac{3}{x} + \dfrac{4}{x} = \dfrac{7}{x}.$

If you used the rule for adding fractions strictly, you would get $\dfrac{7x}{x^2}$ which then cancels to give $\dfrac{7}{x}$. Try it.

(e) $\dfrac{3}{x} + \dfrac{4}{y} = \dfrac{3 \times y + 4 \times x}{xy}$

$\qquad = \dfrac{3y + 4x}{xy}.$

The terms 3y and 4x are unlike, so they cannot be combined.

(f) $2x - \dfrac{5}{y} = \dfrac{2x}{1} - \dfrac{5}{y}$

$\qquad = \dfrac{2x \times y - 5 \times 1}{y}$

$\qquad = \dfrac{2xy - 5}{y}.$

Write $2x = \dfrac{2x}{1}$, and then use the usual rule.

Exercise 5C

1 Carry out the following additions and subtractions, giving your answers as fractions.

(a) $\dfrac{x}{3} + \dfrac{x}{5}$

(b) $\dfrac{y}{2} - \dfrac{y}{5}$

(c) $\frac{2}{3}z - \frac{1}{2}z$

(d) $\dfrac{p}{2} - \dfrac{q}{3}$

(e) $x + \frac{1}{2}y$

(f) $\dfrac{n}{2} + \dfrac{3n}{4}$

(g) $\dfrac{3x}{5} - \dfrac{2x}{15}$

(h) $\dfrac{3y}{4} - \dfrac{2y}{3} - \dfrac{y}{12}$

2 Carry out the following additions and subtractions, giving your answers as fractions.

(a) $\dfrac{2}{x} + \dfrac{3}{x}$

(b) $\dfrac{6}{a} - \dfrac{2}{3a}$

(c) $\dfrac{1}{2p} + \dfrac{2}{3p}$

(d) $\dfrac{5}{y} - \dfrac{1}{8y}$

(e) $\dfrac{5x}{2y} - \dfrac{3x}{4y}$

(f) $\dfrac{2j}{3k} + \dfrac{4j}{6k}$

(g) $\dfrac{a}{5b} - \dfrac{3a}{10b}$

(h) $\dfrac{2}{y} - \dfrac{3}{4y} + \dfrac{1}{2y}$

3 Carry out the following additions and subtractions, giving your answers as fractions.

(a) $\frac{1}{2}a - \frac{1}{2}b$

(b) $\frac{s}{2t} - \frac{t}{s}$

(c) $\frac{u}{v} + \frac{v}{u}$

(d) $\frac{1}{x} + \frac{1}{y} + \frac{1}{z}$

(e) $\frac{3}{x} + \frac{2}{x^2}$

(f) $\frac{x^2}{y} + \frac{y^2}{x}$

(g) $\frac{3x}{y} + \frac{4y}{z}$

(h) $\frac{3}{x} + \frac{x}{2}$

5.6 Some important results to remember

The most important aspect when working with fractions in algebra is to remember that they are treated in the same way as fractions in arithmetic.

Test exercise 5

1 Carry out the following multiplications and divisions, giving your answers as fractions in their lowest terms.

(a) $\frac{5}{6} \times \frac{2}{3}$

(b) $\frac{2}{xy} \times \frac{x}{y^2}$

(c) $\frac{3}{y} \times \frac{2}{x}$

(d) $\frac{x^2}{3} \times \frac{6}{x}$

(e) $\frac{8}{9} \div \frac{16}{27}$

(f) $\frac{x}{2} \div \frac{x^2}{4}$

(g) $\frac{2}{5}a^2 \div \frac{3}{5}a$

(h) $\frac{12x}{7y} \div \frac{3x^2}{14y^2}$

2 Carry out the following calculations, giving your answers as fractions in their lowest terms.

(a) $\frac{5}{6} + \frac{2}{3}$

(b) $\frac{a}{2} + \frac{b}{4}$

(c) $\frac{1}{3x} + \frac{5}{6x}$

(d) $\frac{3p}{q} - \frac{2p}{3q}$

(e) $\frac{1}{n} + \frac{n}{2}$

(f) $\frac{3p}{q} + \frac{q}{p}$

(g) $4 - \frac{5}{x}$

(h) $\frac{3x}{2} - \frac{1}{5x}$

3 Carry out the following calculations, giving your answers as fractions in their lowest terms.

(a) $\frac{1}{2} + \frac{1}{6} - \frac{1}{4}$

(b) $\frac{x}{4} - \frac{x}{2} + \frac{x}{3}$

(c) $\frac{1}{n} + \frac{2}{n} + \frac{3}{n}$

(d) $\frac{p}{2} \times \frac{q}{4}$

(e) $\frac{3}{4}a \div \frac{2}{3}a$

(f) $\frac{1}{2} \times \frac{1}{5} + \frac{1}{3}$

(g) $\frac{x}{4} \times \frac{6}{x^2} - \frac{1}{x}$

(h) $\frac{a}{3} + \frac{b}{2} \times \frac{3a}{b}$

6 Indices

This chapter extends the notation x^2 and x^3 introduced in Chapter 1. When you have completed it you should

- know how to use indices for multiplication and division of powers.

6.1 Index notation

In Section 1.3, you saw that $x \times x$ is written as x^2, and $x \times x \times x$ is written as x^3.

This suggests the notation $x \times x \times x \times x = x^4$, $x \times x \times x \times x \times x = x^5$, and so on. These are read as 'x to the **power** 4' (or 'x to the fourth), 'x to the power 5', and so on. On its own the power is called an **index**; the plural form of index is **indices**. In the expression x^4, x is called the **base**, and 4 is the index.

This way of writing powers, called **index notation**, enables you to multiply and divide powers of numbers quickly.

Note that in index notation x^1 means x.

Example 6.1.1
Simplify the following, giving your answers in index form.

(a) $3^3 \times 3^2$ (b) 2×2^3 (c) $5^5 \div 5^2$ (d) $\dfrac{2^2}{2^5}$

(a) $3^3 \times 3^2 = (3 \times 3 \times 3) \times (3 \times 3)$ *The meaning of 3^3 and 3^2.*

$\qquad\qquad = 3 \times 3 \times 3 \times 3 \times 3$ *Brackets not needed for multiplying.*

$\qquad\qquad = 3^5.$ *The meaning of 3^5.*

(b) $2 \times 2^3 = (2) \times (2 \times 2 \times 2)$ *Recall that $2 = 2^1$.*

$\qquad\qquad = 2 \times 2 \times 2 \times 2 = 2^4.$

(c) $5^5 \div 5^2 = \dfrac{5 \times 5 \times 5 \times 5 \times 5}{5 \times 5}$ *Fraction notation is often clearer than using a division sign.*

$\qquad\quad = \dfrac{\cancel{5} \times \cancel{5} \times 5 \times 5 \times 5}{\cancel{5} \times \cancel{5}} = 5^3.$ *Cancelling the 5s leaves 5^3.*

(d) $\dfrac{2^2}{2^5} = \dfrac{2 \times 2}{2 \times 2 \times 2 \times 2 \times 2}$

$\qquad\quad = \dfrac{\cancel{2} \times \cancel{2}}{\cancel{2} \times \cancel{2} \times 2 \times 2 \times 2} = \dfrac{1}{2^3}.$ *Cancelling the 2s, leaves 2^3 in the denominator so the result is $\dfrac{1}{2^3}$.*

Example 6.1.1 suggests two rules for indices.

6.2 Rules for indices

Addition rule for multiplication

Example 6.1.1 (a) and (b) suggest that when you multiply powers of the same number, you add the indices.

$$x^m \times x^n = x^{m+n}.$$

Subtraction rule for division

Example 6.1.1 (c) and (d), which give the results $\dfrac{5^5}{5^2} = 5^3$ and $\dfrac{2^2}{2^5} = \dfrac{1}{2^3}$, suggest that dividing is closely related to subtracting the indices. The following rule looks complicated but is easy to use.

$$\frac{x^m}{x^n} = \begin{cases} x^{m-n} & \text{if } m \text{ is bigger than } n, \\ \dfrac{1}{x^{n-m}} & \text{if } n \text{ is bigger than } m. \end{cases}$$

Example 6.2.1

Simplify   (a) $x^3 \times x^2$,   (b) $y^8 \div y^3$,   (c) $\dfrac{z^3}{z^7}$,   (d) $\dfrac{t^3 \times t^4}{t^6}$,   (e) $\left(x^3\right)^2$.

(a) $x^3 \times x^2 = x^{3+2} = x^5$.   *Use the addition rule.*

(b) $y^8 \div y^3 = \dfrac{y^8}{y^3}$ *Change to fraction form.*

                     Use the subtraction rule, first part.

      $= y^{8-3} = y^5$.

(c) $\dfrac{z^3}{z^7} = \dfrac{1}{z^{7-3}} = \dfrac{1}{z^4}$.   *Use the subtraction rule, second part.*

(d) $\dfrac{t^3 \times t^4}{t^6} = \dfrac{t^{3+4}}{t^6}$ *Use the addition rule.*

      $= \dfrac{t^7}{t^6}$ *Use the subtraction rule, and the fact that $t^1 = t$.*

      $= t^1 = t$.

(e) $\left(x^3\right)^2 = x^3 \times x^3 = x^6$.   *Use the addition rule.*

You may have noticed that you could do part (d) of Example 6.2.1 in one operation by combining the addition and subtraction rules and saying that

$$\frac{t^3 \times t^4}{t^6} = t^{3+4-6} = t^1 = t.$$

████ **Exercise 6A** ████

1 Simplify each of the following, leaving your answer in index form.

(a) $2^3 \times 2^4$ (b) $4^3 \times 4^4$ (c) $3^2 \times 3 \times 3^3$

(d) $5^5 \div 5^2$ (e) $2^2 \div 2^4$ (f) $7^3 \times 7^2 \div 7^4$

(g) $\dfrac{2^3 \times 2^7}{2^4}$ (h) $\dfrac{3^4 \times 3^5}{3^{10}}$ (i) $\dfrac{3^4 \times 3^5}{3^2 \times 3^3}$

2 Simplify each of the following, leaving your answer in index form.

(a) $x^5 \times x^4$ (b) $x \times x^4 \times x^3$ (c) $y^2 \div y^7$

(d) $p^4 \times p^2 \div p^3$ (e) $\left(q^4 \times q^2\right) \div \left(q^3 \times q\right)$ (f) $\left(r^2 \times r^2\right) \div r^6$

(g) $\dfrac{t \times t^2}{t^4}$ (h) $\dfrac{x^2 \times x^4}{x^3 \times x^5}$ (i) $\dfrac{y^5 \times y^3}{y^4 \times y^4}$

3 Simplify each of the following, leaving your answer in index form.

(a) $\left(2^2\right)^3$ (b) $\left(3^3\right)^4$ (c) $\left(5^2\right)^4$

(d) $\left(x^5\right)^3$ (e) $\left(y^3\right)^2$ (f) $\left(z^4\right)^5$

6.3 The third index rule

Look for a pattern in your answers to Exercise 6A Question 3.

All the parts have the same form: a power is raised to a power.

The 'power-on-power' rule

Exercise 6A Question 3 suggests that when you raise a power to a power, you multiply the indices.

$$\left(x^m\right)^n = x^{mn}.$$

Example 6.3.1

Simplify   (a) $\left(x^2\right)^6$,   (b) $\dfrac{1}{\left(y^3\right)^5}$.

(a) $\left(x^2\right)^6 = x^{2 \times 6} = x^{12}$.   *Use the power-on-power rule.*

(b) $\dfrac{1}{\left(y^3\right)^5} = \dfrac{1}{y^{3\times5}} = \dfrac{1}{y^{15}}$.   *Use the power-on-power rule.*

▓▓▓▓▓▓▓▓▓▓▓▓▓▓▓▓▓▓▓▓▓▓▓▓▓   **Exercise 6B**   ▓▓▓▓▓▓▓▓▓▓▓▓▓

1 Simplify each of the following, leaving your answer in index form.

(a) $\left(2^2\right)^9$

(b) $\left(3^4\right)^2$

(c) $\left(5^5\right)^5$

(d) $\left(p^2\right)^5$

(e) $\left(q^3\right)^6$

(f) $\left(r^6\right)^2$

(g) $\dfrac{1}{\left(s^2\right)^7}$

(h) $\dfrac{1}{\left(t^3\right)^8}$

(i) $\dfrac{1}{\left(u^4\right)^8}$

(j) $\dfrac{x^5}{\left(x^3\right)^2}$

(k) $\dfrac{\left(y^6\right)^2}{\left(y^2\right)^5}$

(l) $\dfrac{\left(z^4\right)^4}{\left(z^2\right)^2 \times \left(z^3\right)^3}$

(m) $\dfrac{x^3 \times \left(x^2\right)^4}{\left(x^4\right)^2 \times x^2}$

(n) $\dfrac{y \times y^3 \times \left(y^3\right)^4}{\left(y^2\right)^2 \times y^2}$

(o) $\dfrac{z \times z^2 \times \left(z^5\right)^4}{\left(z^2\right)^5 \times z \times z^2}$

6.4 Mixed bases

What happens if you mix the bases in an expression, so that you have different numbers with indices? Example 6.4.1 shows you what to do.

Example 6.4.1
Simplify

(a) $\left(2^2 \times 3\right) \times \left(2^4 \times 3^3\right)$,   (b) $\left(2x^3 y\right) \times \left(3x^2 y^2\right)$,   (c) $\left(\dfrac{2x^3}{y^2}\right)^2$.

(a) $\left(2^2 \times 3\right) \times \left(2^4 \times 3^3\right) = 2^2 \times 3 \times 2^4 \times 3^3$ *Brackets are unnecessary.*

$= 2^2 \times 2^4 \times 3 \times 3^3$ *The order in which you multiply is not important.*

$= 2^6 \times 3^4$.

(b) $\left(2x^3 y\right) \times \left(3x^2 y^2\right) = 2 \times x^3 \times y \times 3 \times x^2 \times y^2$ *Brackets are unnecessary.*

$= 2 \times 3 \times x^3 \times x^2 \times y \times y^2$ *The order in which you multiply is not important.*

$= 6 \times x^5 \times y^3 = 6x^5 y^3$.

(c) $\left(\dfrac{2x^3}{y^2}\right)^2 = \dfrac{2x^3}{y^2} \times \dfrac{2x^3}{y^2} = \dfrac{2 \times x^3 \times 2 \times x^3}{y^2 \times y^2}$

$= \dfrac{2 \times 2 \times x^3 \times x^3}{y^2 \times y^2} = \dfrac{4x^6}{y^4}$.   *The order in which you multiply is not important.*

You can shorten the working in the three parts of Example 6.4.1.

Work out the final number and the powers of the various letters separately.

Start by finding the number, and then consider the letters in turn.

Here is how you might write a solution in shortened form.

Example 6.4.2
Simplify the following.

(a) $\left(3a^2b^4\right) \times \left(5ab^3\right)$ (b) $\left(2x^3y\right) \div \left(6x^2y^2\right)$ (c) $\dfrac{3c^2d}{d^3} \div \dfrac{9c}{d^2}$

(d) $\left(6x^2y\right)^3$ (e) $\dfrac{\left(2c^2d^3\right)^3}{4cd \times 8cd^2}$ (f) $\dfrac{2p^2q}{5pq^4} \times \dfrac{\left(10p^2q\right)^3}{25pq \times 8(pq)^2}$

(a) $\left(3a^2b^4\right) \times \left(5ab^3\right) = 15a^3b^7$.

> The number and the powers of a and b are considered separately.

(b) $\left(2x^3y\right) \div \left(6x^2y^2\right) = \dfrac{2x^3y}{6x^2y^2}$

> Write in fraction form first.

$\qquad = \dfrac{1x}{3y} = \dfrac{x}{3y}$.

> The 1 in the top line can be left out.

(c) $\dfrac{3c^2d}{d^3} \div \dfrac{9c}{d^2} = \dfrac{3c^2d}{d^3} \times \dfrac{d^2}{9c} = \dfrac{c}{3}$.

> To divide by a fraction, turn it upside down and multiply.

(d) $\left(6x^2y\right)^3 = 6x^2y \times 6x^2y \times 6x^2y$

> It is usual to omit this first step.

$\qquad = 6^3 \times \left(x^2\right)^3 \times y^3$

> Use the power-on-power rule.

$\qquad = 216x^6y^3$.

> Remember to cube the 6.

(e) $\dfrac{\left(2c^2d^3\right)^3}{4cd \times 8cd^2} = \dfrac{8c^6d^9}{4cd \times 8cd^2}$

> Use the power-on-power rule for the top line, and write 2^3 as 8.

$\qquad = \dfrac{1c^4d^6}{4} = \dfrac{c^4d^6}{4}$.

> The 1 in the top line can be left out.

(f) $\dfrac{2p^2q}{5pq^4} \times \dfrac{\left(10p^2q\right)^3}{25pq \times 8(pq)^2}$

$\qquad = \dfrac{2p^2q}{5pq^4} \times \dfrac{1000p^6q^3}{25pq \times 8p^2q^2}$

> Use the power-on-power rule for the expressions in brackets.

$\qquad = \dfrac{2p^4}{q^3}$.

Exercise 6C

1 Simplify each of the following.

(a) $2pq \times 4p^2q^3$

(b) $3s^2t \times 15s^2t$

(c) $8x^2yz \times 3xy^2z^3$

(d) $\dfrac{32a^4b^4}{12ab^5}$

(e) $\dfrac{24m^2n^4}{32m^3n^7}$

(f) $\dfrac{18u^6v^3}{27v^3u^2}$

(g) $\left(6a^3b^2\right) \div (2ab)$

(h) $\left(4k^3l^2\right) \div \left(10kl^3\right)$

(i) $\left(14ef^2\right) \div \left(21f^3e\right)$

(j) $\left(2x^2y^3\right)^3$

(k) $\left(4p \div q^3\right)^3$

(l) $\left(3c^2 \div cd^3\right)^2$

2 Simplify the following expressions.

(a) $\dfrac{4x^2y}{3xy^4} \times \dfrac{6x^2y^3}{2x^4y}$

(b) $\dfrac{5p^2}{4p^3q^4} \times \dfrac{8p^4q}{25q^4p}$

(c) $\left(\dfrac{2a}{b}\right)^2 \div \dfrac{a^2}{b^3}$

(d) $\dfrac{3st}{(2s^2t)^2} \times \dfrac{2s}{3t}$

(e) $\left(\dfrac{3r^2s}{2rs^3}\right)^2 \times \dfrac{r}{6s}$

(f) $\dfrac{2u}{3v^2} \div \dfrac{4v^2}{3u^2v^3}$

(g) $\dfrac{2m^2}{3l} \div \left(\dfrac{2l}{3m}\right)^2$

(h) $\dfrac{2e}{f} \times \dfrac{e^2f}{3} \times \left(\dfrac{e}{f}\right)^2$

(i) $\left(\dfrac{2x^2y}{3z}\right)^2 \times \dfrac{z^2}{3y^2} \times \dfrac{1}{x}$

(j) $\dfrac{2p}{3q^2} \times \left(\dfrac{3q}{2r}\right)^3 \div \dfrac{2r^3}{3p^2}$

(k) $\left(\dfrac{x}{y}\right)^2 \times \left(\dfrac{y}{z}\right)^2 \div \left(\dfrac{x}{z}\right)^2$

(l) $\left(\dfrac{2a}{b}\right)^3 \div \left(\dfrac{a}{2c^2}\right)^2$

3 Expand the brackets and simplify the following expressions.

(a) $(4x)^2 - (3x)^2$

(b) $(-3y)^2 - 3y^2$

(c) $4z^2 - (-2z)^2$

(d) $4z^3 - (-2z)^3$

(e) $-(2x)^3 - (-2x)^3$

(f) $\left(3x^2\right)^2 + (-x)^4$

(g) $5a^3 + (-2a)^3$

(h) $-\left(-2x^2\right)^3 - \left(-3x^3\right)^2$

(i) $-(-2x)^5 + (2x)^5$

6.5 Some important results to remember

Work out the final number and the powers of the various letters separately.

Addition rule for multiplication

$$x^m \times x^n = x^{m+n}.$$

Subtraction rule for division

$$\frac{x^m}{x^n} = \begin{cases} x^{m-n} & \text{if } m \text{ is bigger than } n, \\ \dfrac{1}{x^{n-m}} & \text{if } n \text{ is bigger than } m. \end{cases}$$

The power-on-power rule

$$\left(x^m\right)^n = x^{mn}.$$

Test exercise 6

1 Simplify the following.

(a) $\left(2^2 \times 3 \times 5^2\right) \times \left(2 \times 3^2 \times 5^3\right)$

(b) $\left(2^2 \times 3 \times 5^2\right) \div \left(2 \times 3^2 \times 5^3\right)$

(c) $\dfrac{2x}{3y} \times \dfrac{6y}{z^2} \times \dfrac{z^3}{2x^3}$

(d) $\left(\dfrac{2a}{3b}\right)^2 \times \left(\dfrac{3b}{c}\right)^3$

(e) $\left(\dfrac{3r^2}{2s}\right)^3 \div \left(\dfrac{3s}{4t}\right)^2$

(f) $\left(\dfrac{2l}{3m}\right)^3 \times \left(\dfrac{mn}{2l}\right)^2 \div \left(\dfrac{6lm}{n^3}\right)^2$

7 Brackets and fractions in equations

In Chapter 5, all the fractions had, to start with, just a single term in the numerator. This chapter involves no new ideas, but it brings together a number of the techniques you have learned so far. When you have completed it you should be able to

- handle fractions which include brackets
- handle multiplication of fractions which include brackets
- solve equations which include fractions and brackets.

7.1 More complicated additions and subtractions

If you have to work with a fraction such as $\dfrac{x+1}{2}$, and you wish to find its value when $x = 5$, the calculation you would carry out is

$$\frac{5+1}{2} = \frac{6}{2} = 3.$$

What you have done is to add the x and the 1, that is add the 5 and 1 first, and then divide by the 2.

This is the same as saying that $x + 1$ is in brackets. In effect the fraction bar, that is the line between the numerator and the denominator, acts as a bracket.

This is extremely important.

So, when you see $\dfrac{x+1}{2}$, it is worth writing it as $\dfrac{(x+1)}{2}$ as a reminder.

Similarly, you should write $\frac{1}{2}(x+1)$ as $\dfrac{(x+1)}{2}$.

And the same applies when you see a fraction like $\frac{3}{5}(x+1)$. Write it as $\dfrac{3(x+1)}{5}$.

The only other thing to remember is that fractions in algebra are just the same as fractions in arithmetic, and you will need to use the rules for adding or subtracting fractions in Section 4.6.

These are

$$\frac{a}{b} + \frac{c}{d} = \frac{ad+cb}{bd} \qquad \text{and} \qquad \frac{a}{b} - \frac{c}{d} = \frac{ad-cb}{bd}.$$

Example 7.1.1

Express as single fractions　(a) $\dfrac{x+1}{2}+\dfrac{x+2}{3}$,　(b) $\dfrac{x+1}{2}-\dfrac{x+2}{3}$,

(c) $\dfrac{3}{2}(x+1)-\dfrac{5}{7}(x-2)$.

(a)
$$\dfrac{x+1}{2}+\dfrac{x+2}{3}=\dfrac{(x+1)}{2}+\dfrac{(x+2)}{3}$$
$$=\dfrac{(x+1)\times3+(x+2)\times2}{2\times3}$$
$$=\dfrac{3(x+1)+2(x+2)}{6}$$
$$=\dfrac{3x+3+2x+4}{6}=\dfrac{5x+7}{6}.$$

This first step is the key to handling fractions like these correctly. Put in the brackets.

Everything else follows the standard rules.

(b)
$$\dfrac{x+1}{2}-\dfrac{x+2}{3}=\dfrac{(x+1)}{2}-\dfrac{(x+2)}{3}$$
$$=\dfrac{(x+1)\times3-(x+2)\times2}{2\times3}$$
$$=\dfrac{3(x+1)-2(x+2)}{6}$$
$$=\dfrac{3x+3-2x-4}{6}=\dfrac{x-1}{6}.$$

Part (b) is like part (a), except for the sign.

If you put in the brackets correctly, you should be able to deal with the negative sign between the fractions.

(c)
$$\dfrac{3}{2}(x+1)-\dfrac{5}{7}(x-2)=\dfrac{3(x+1)}{2}-\dfrac{5(x-2)}{7}$$
$$=\dfrac{3(x+1)\times7-5(x-2)\times2}{2\times7}$$
$$=\dfrac{21(x+1)-10(x-2)}{14}$$
$$=\dfrac{21x+21-10x+20}{14}$$
$$=\dfrac{11x+41}{14}.$$

Note the extra first step.

$3(x+1)\times7$ is the same as $3\times(x+1)\times7$ which is $21(x+1)$.

Note that minus times minus equals plus has been used to get $+20$.

Exercise 7A

1 Express each of the following as single fractions.

(a) $\dfrac{x+1}{3}+\dfrac{x+2}{4}$

(b) $\dfrac{2x-1}{2}+\dfrac{3x+2}{3}$

(c) $\dfrac{4x-1}{3}+\dfrac{2x-3}{2}$

(d) $\dfrac{x+1}{3}-\dfrac{x+2}{4}$

(e) $\dfrac{2x+4}{2}-\dfrac{3x+2}{3}$

(f) $\dfrac{4x-1}{3}-\dfrac{2x-3}{2}$

(g) $\dfrac{x+2y}{3}+\dfrac{2x-3y}{4}$

(h) $\dfrac{x+2y}{3}-\dfrac{2x-3y}{4}$

(i) $\dfrac{x}{4}+\dfrac{x-2y}{12}-\dfrac{2x-y}{6}$

2 Express each of the following as single fractions.

(a) $\dfrac{5(1+x)}{6}+\dfrac{(1+2x)}{4}$ (b) $\dfrac{3(2-x)}{4}-\dfrac{3(x-5)}{5}$ (c) $\dfrac{5x}{6}-\dfrac{(2x+3)}{4}$

(d) $\frac{3}{2}(1+x)+\frac{2}{3}(2-x)$ (e) $\frac{4}{5}(2-3x)-\frac{1}{2}(2+5x)$ (f) $\frac{2}{3}x-\frac{2}{3}(1+x)$

(g) $\frac{2}{5}(x+4)-\frac{1}{4}(x+2)$ (h) $\frac{3}{7}(x+4y)-\frac{5}{2}x+\frac{3}{4}y$ (i) $\dfrac{2(3-x)}{3}-\dfrac{3+x}{4}$

7.2 More complicated multiplications

When solving equations involving fractions it is helpful to start by changing the equation into one without fractions, and then to use the techniques of Chapter 3. This section gives practice at multiplying a fraction by a single number to obtain an algebraic expression without fractions.

Example 7.2.1

Multiply   (a) $\dfrac{x}{3}$ by 6,   (b) $\frac{1}{5}x$ by 15.

(a) $6\times\dfrac{x}{3}=\dfrac{6}{1}\times\dfrac{x}{3}=\dfrac{6\times x}{1\times 3}=\dfrac{6x}{3}$

$\qquad\qquad = 2x.$

The number 6 is the fraction $\dfrac{6}{1}$.

The 3 cancels, leaving $2x$.

(b) $15\times\frac{1}{5}x=15\times\dfrac{x}{5}$

$\qquad =\dfrac{15}{1}\times\dfrac{x}{5}=\dfrac{15\times x}{1\times 5}$

$\qquad = 3x.$

$\frac{1}{5}x$ means $\dfrac{x}{5}$.

The rest of the argument is similar to that for part (a).

Look carefully at the examples above. The solutions have been shown in detail although the answers should have been obvious. Here are some harder examples where some of the steps have been left out.

Example 7.2.2

Multiply   (a) $\dfrac{4x-1}{3}$ by 12,   (b) $\frac{1}{4}(3x-7)$ by 8.

(a) $12\times\dfrac{4x-1}{3}=\dfrac{12(4x-1)}{3}$

$\qquad = 4(4x-1)$

$\qquad = 16x-4.$

Fraction bars act as brackets; put in the brackets.

Now cancel the factor of 3.

Then multiply out the bracket.

(b) $8 \times \frac{1}{4}(3x-7) = 8 \times \dfrac{3x-7}{4}$

$\qquad = \dfrac{8(3x-7)}{4}$

$\qquad = 2(3x-7)$

$\qquad = 6x-14.$

In future the first step will be left out.

This is now similar to part (a).

Example 7.2.3

Multiply   (a) $\dfrac{4x-1}{3} + \dfrac{2x-3}{2}$ by 6,   (b) $\dfrac{5x+3}{4} - \dfrac{3x-1}{2}$ by 4.

(a) $6\left(\dfrac{4x-1}{3} + \dfrac{2x-3}{2}\right) = 6 \times \dfrac{4x-1}{3} + 6 \times \dfrac{2x-3}{2}$

$\qquad = \dfrac{6(4x-1)}{3} + \dfrac{6(2x-3)}{2}$

$\qquad = 2(4x-1) + 3(2x-3)$

$\qquad = 8x-2+6x-9$

$\qquad = 14x-11.$

Multiply both terms by 6.

Fraction bars act as brackets; put in the brackets. Then cancel.

Multiply out the brackets, collect like terms and simplify.

(b) $4\left(\dfrac{5x+3}{4} - \dfrac{3x-1}{2}\right) = \dfrac{4(5x+3)}{4} - \dfrac{4(3x-1)}{2}$

$\qquad = 1(5x+3) - 2(3x-1)$

$\qquad = 5x+3-6x+2$

$\qquad = -x+5.$

Multiply both terms by 4, then cancel.

The brackets should help you to get the signs correct.

Finally collect like terms.

You may have wondered why, in Example 7.2.3, the numbers 6 and 4 were chosen as the numbers to multiply by.

In Example 7.2.3(a), 6 is the smallest number which both 3 and 2 divide into exactly. In fact, 6 is the lowest common multiple of 3 and 2.

In Example 7.2.3(b), 4 is the smallest number that both 4 and 2 divide into exactly. In fact, 4 is the lowest common multiple of 4 and 2.

Exercise 7B

1 Simplify the following.

(a) $4 \times \dfrac{x}{2}$ (b) $\frac{1}{2}x \times 16$ (c) $3 \times \dfrac{y}{3}$ (d) $14 \times \frac{1}{7}p$

(e) $6 \times \dfrac{q+4}{3}$ (f) $8 \times \frac{1}{4}(a+3)$ (g) $3 \times \frac{1}{3}(2r-7)$ (h) $10 \times \dfrac{5t-7}{2}$

2 In each part multiply the expression by the given number and simplify your answer.

(a) $\dfrac{x-1}{2}+\dfrac{x+1}{4}, \quad 4$

(b) $\dfrac{2x+1}{6}+\dfrac{x-1}{3}, \quad 6$

(c) $\dfrac{2x-1}{4}-\dfrac{x-1}{4}, \quad 4$

(d) $\dfrac{3s+2}{4}-\dfrac{2s+3}{3}, \quad 12$

(e) $\dfrac{3t-1}{3}-\dfrac{6t-1}{6}, \quad 6$

(f) $\dfrac{v-1}{3}-\dfrac{v+1}{3}, \quad 3$

(g) $t-\dfrac{3t+4}{4}, \quad 4$

(h) $\dfrac{3t-2}{5}-1+t, \quad 5$

(i) $\dfrac{q+1}{2}-\dfrac{q-1}{2}-1, \quad 2$

7.3 Equations involving fractions

All the equations which you met in Chapter 3 involved only whole numbers. In this section you will tackle equations which include fractions.

Remember Rule 3 on page 18 which states that "You can multiply or divide both sides of an equation by the same number."

In the following examples, both sides of the equations will be multiplied by the same number to obtain a new equation without fractions.

Example 7.3.1

Solve the equations   (a) $\dfrac{x}{6}=2$,   (b) $\dfrac{1}{3}x=\dfrac{3}{4}$,   (c) $\dfrac{3x+2}{3}=\dfrac{2x+1}{6}$.

(a) $\quad \dfrac{x}{6}=2$

$\dfrac{6}{1}\times\dfrac{x}{6}=6\times 2$

$x=12.$

It is a good idea to try to get rid of fractions. In this case, multiply both sides of the equation by 6 which is the same as $\dfrac{6}{1}$.

(b) $\quad \dfrac{1}{3}x=\dfrac{3}{4}$

$\dfrac{x}{3}=\dfrac{3}{4}$

$\dfrac{12}{1}\times\dfrac{x}{3}=\dfrac{12}{1}\times\dfrac{3}{4}$

$\dfrac{12x}{3}=\dfrac{36}{4}$

$4x=9$

$x=\dfrac{9}{4}.$

Rewrite in fraction notation.

Multiply by 12. Then cancel to get rid of the fractions.

In this particular case you could have started by multiplying both sides by 3 and obtained the final result more quickly

(c) $\dfrac{3x+2}{3} = \dfrac{2x+1}{6}$

$\dfrac{6(3x+2)}{3} = \dfrac{6(2x+1)}{6}$

$2(3x+2) = 1(2x+1)$

$6x+4 = 2x+1$

$4x = -3$

$x = -\dfrac{3}{4}.$

Put in the brackets. Multiply both sides by 6. *Then cancel to get rid of the fractions.*

Expand the brackets.

This is now in familiar form.

Notice how the aim is to get the equation into a form without fractions and brackets, because it is then in a familiar form which you know how to solve.

Use the smallest possible number for multiplying: this will keep the size of all the numbers as small as possible.

Example 7.3.2 shows two more cases of multiplying to get rid of fractions.

Example 7.3.2

Solve the equations   (a) $1 + \dfrac{x+6}{7} = \dfrac{x+1}{3}$,   (b) $\tfrac{3}{4}(x+1) - \tfrac{8}{3}(2x+7) = 5$.

(a) $1 + \dfrac{x+6}{7} = \dfrac{x+1}{3}$

$21 + \dfrac{21(x+6)}{7} = \dfrac{21(x+1)}{3}$

$21 + 3(x+6) = 7(x+1)$

$21 + 3x + 18 = 7x + 7$

$-4x = -32$

$x = 8.$

Put in the brackets.

Multiply both sides by 21. *Don't forget to multiply the* 1. *Then cancel.*

Expand the brackets.

This is now in familiar form.

(b) $\tfrac{3}{4}(x+1) - \tfrac{8}{3}(2x+7) = 5$

$\dfrac{3(x+1)}{4} - \dfrac{8(2x+7)}{3} = 5$

$\dfrac{12 \times 3(x+1)}{4} - \dfrac{12 \times 8(2x+7)}{3} = 60$

$9(x+1) - 32(2x+7) = 60$

$9x + 9 - 64x - 224 = 60$

$-55x = 275$

$x = -5.$

Write in fraction form.

Multiply both sides by 12 *remembering to put in the brackets where necessary. Then cancel.*

Expand the brackets.

This is now in familiar form.

Checking your answers

When you have solved an equation it is good practice to check your solution. You can do this by substituting your solution into the original equation.

Here is an example.

Suppose that you have solved the equation

$$\tfrac{1}{3}(x+2)+\tfrac{1}{2}(x-1)=\tfrac{1}{5}(3x-1)+2$$

and got the solution $x = 7$.

Substitute $x = 7$ in the left side.

$$\text{Left side} = \tfrac{1}{3}\times 9 + \tfrac{1}{2}\times 6 = 3+3 = 6.$$

Substitute $x = 7$ in the right side.

$$\text{Right side} = \tfrac{1}{5}\times 20 + 2 = 4+2 = 6.$$

As the left and right sides are equal, the solution is correct.

In practice, you can often check your solution mentally.

Exercise 7C

1   Solve the following equations, checking your solutions.

(a) $\dfrac{x}{4}=\dfrac{5}{3}$ (b) $\dfrac{y}{3}=2$ (c) $4z=\dfrac{3}{2}$ (d) $\tfrac{1}{3}t=\dfrac{5}{3}$

(e) $\dfrac{x}{3}=\dfrac{x}{4}+1$ (f) $\tfrac{1}{2}y=3-2y$ (g) $\tfrac{3}{2}z=\dfrac{4}{3}-\dfrac{5}{4}z$ (h) $t=\dfrac{3}{2}+\dfrac{2}{3}t$

2   Solve the following equations, checking your solutions.

(a) $\dfrac{x-1}{2}=\dfrac{3}{4}$ (b) $\dfrac{2y-3}{9}=\dfrac{1}{3}$ (c) $\dfrac{3z-1}{4}=\dfrac{z}{2}$

(d) $\dfrac{t}{2}-\dfrac{t+2}{3}=0$ (e) $\tfrac{1}{3}(2x-3)=x$ (f) $5-\tfrac{1}{4}(7p-1)=0$

3   Solve the following equations, checking your solutions.

(a) $\tfrac{1}{3}(4a-1)+\tfrac{1}{2}(a-14)=0$ (b) $\tfrac{1}{3}(4a-1)-\tfrac{1}{2}(a-4)=0$

(c) $\dfrac{x-1}{2}+\dfrac{x+1}{2}=3$ (d) $\dfrac{3x-1}{2}-\dfrac{x+1}{2}=3$

(e) $\tfrac{1}{6}(5a-7)+\tfrac{1}{9}(5a+2)=6$ (f) $\tfrac{1}{2}(1-s)-\tfrac{1}{3}(2s-1)=2$

(g) $\dfrac{x+2}{3}+\dfrac{x+3}{4}=\dfrac{2(x+4)}{5}$ (h) $\tfrac{1}{2}y-\tfrac{1}{3}(2y+5)=-2$

7.4 Some important results to remember

In a fraction the bar acts as a bracket.

When manipulating fractions, put in brackets as soon as possible.

Use the following rules:

Rule 1
You can add or subtract equal quantities from both sides of an equation.

Rule 2
You can swap the two sides of an equation.

Rule 3
You can multiply or divide both sides of an equation by the same number.

If there are brackets, you should expand them.

At any stage you can simplify either side of the equation.

Test exercise 7

1 Solve the following equations, checking that your answers are correct.

(a) $2 - x = 3$ 　　　　(b) $4 + 2z = -10$ 　　　　(c) $1 - 3z = 15 + 4z$

(d) $2 = 4k - 3 + k$ 　　　(e) $-3u + 2 = 2 + u$ 　　　(f) $2v - 7 = 2 + v$

2 Find the solution of each of the following equations. In each case, check your answers.

(a) $2(w - 3) = 10$ 　　　　　　　　(b) $5(x - 1) = 2(x + 2)$

(c) $4 - 2y = 3(1 - y)$ 　　　　　　(d) $4c + 3(2 - 3c) = 16$

(e) $5(2 - t) = 2(t - 1) + 4(t + 3)$ 　　(f) $2(h + 1) - 4(h - 1) = -2 + 3(h - 4)$

3 Find the solution of each of the following equations.

(a) $\dfrac{1 - 2x}{3} - \dfrac{1 + 3x}{4} = 10$ 　　　　　　(b) $\dfrac{x}{6} - \dfrac{x - 2}{3} = 4$

(c) $\frac{2}{3}(x + 1) - \frac{3}{5}(2x - 3) = \frac{1}{3}$ 　　　　(d) $\frac{4}{7}(2x - 1) - \frac{1}{2}(x - 5) = 2$

(e) $\dfrac{1 + 2x}{5} - \dfrac{5 + 3x}{4} = \dfrac{x - 4}{2} - 5$ 　　　(f) $\frac{2}{3}(x + 4) - \frac{3}{4}(2x + 5) = \frac{1}{12}(x - 2)$

8 Factorising and brackets

In Chapter 2, you learned how to multiply out brackets, that is to expand them. This chapter is about the reverse process. When you have completed it you should

- be able to factorise simple expressions.

8.1 Factors

When you have an expression such as $3(x+2)$ where two things are multiplied together, in this case 3 and $x+2$, the expression is said to be in **factor form**, or **factorised**. The numbers 3 and $x+2$ are the **factors** of $3(x+2)$.

So $3(x+2)$ is in factor form, but $3x+6$ is not.

The process of writing $3x+6$ in the form $3(x+2)$ is called **factorising**.

Factorising expressions can be useful.

Example 8.1.1
Factorise   (a) $4x+10$,   (b) $5y-10$,   (c) $-2z+4$,   (d) $-3t-6$.

(a) $4x+10 = 2(2x+5)$ *The number 2 divides into both terms of $4x+10$.*

(b) $5y-10 = 5(y-2)$ *Notice the signs on both sides.*

(c) $-2z+4 = -2(z-2)$ *Notice the signs again.*

(d) $-3t-6 = -3(t+2)$ *Take care with the signs. You could also write $3(-t-2)$.*

The best way to check the sign in the brackets is to expand your answer to see if you get the expression with which you started.

Example 8.1.2
Factorise $4a+8$.

$$4a+8 = 2(2a+4)$$
$$= 4(a+2).$$

$2(2a+4)$ is not completely factorised because $2a+4$ can be factorised as $2(a+2)$.

$4(a+2)$ is completely factorised.

In Example 8.1.2, $2(2a+4)$ is not completely factorised because the terms in brackets, $2a$ and 4, have a common factor: 2 divides into both $2a$ and 4. The expression $4a+8 = 4(a+2)$ is **completely factorised**.

You should always look for as many factors as possible and factorise completely.

In Examples 8.1.1 and 8.1.2 the common factors are all numbers. Common factors can also be letters, or combinations of letters, as in the following example.

Example 8.1.3
Factorise completely (a) $ab+ac$, (b) $-pq+p^2q$.

(a) $ab+ac = a(b+c)$ *a divides both terms of $ab+ac$.*

(b) $-pq+p^2q = -pq(1-p)$ *pq divides both terms.*

Exercise 8A

1 Factorise the following expressions.

   (a) $3p+9$ (b) $2q-6$ (c) $10r+12$ (d) $3s-15$

   (e) $-2a+14$ (f) $-4b-6$ (g) $-8c+6$ (h) $-9d-3$

2 Factorise the following expressions completely.

   (a) $8x+16$ (b) $9y+18$ (c) $4z-8$ (d) $8t-8$

   (e) $-8x-4$ (f) $-81y+18$ (g) $-4z-2$ (h) $-16t-4$

3 Factorise each of the following expressions completely.

   (a) x^2+2x (b) $2x^2-x$ (c) $-x-x^2$ (d) x^2-xz

   (e) x^2-3xz (f) $-x^2+kx$ (g) $ab+bx$ (h) ax^2+bx

8.2 Expanding $(a+b)(x+y)$

So far, all the brackets in this book have been of the form $z(a+b)$ or $(a+b)z$, where z is a number, which you have expanded in the form $z(a+b)=za+zb$ or $(a+b)z=az+bz$. These expressions are of course all equal to each other.

Now suppose that, instead of a number, $z=x+y$, so that $(a+b)z$ becomes $(a+b)(x+y)$ and you are expanding one bracket multiplied by another.

Then

$$(a+b)(x+y)=a(x+y)+b(x+y)$$
$$= ax+ay+bx+by.$$

This is the same as $(a+b)z=az+bz$ with $x+y$ replacing z.

Expand the brackets.

You do not need to write out all this when you expand brackets.

If you examine

$$(a+b)(x+y)= ax+ay+bx+by.$$

every term in the first bracket multiplies
every term in the second (and vice versa).
The results are then added.

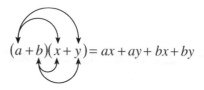

$$(a+b)(x+y)= ax+ay+bx+by$$

Example 8.2.1

Expand the following brackets.

(a) $(p+q)(r+s)$ (b) $(a-2)(b+3)$ (c) $(x+2)(x+3)$ (d) $(x+2)(x-4)$

(a) $(p+q)(r+s)= pr+ ps+ qr+ qs.$

(b) $(a-2)(b+3)= ab+3a-2b-6$.

(c) $(x+2)(x+3)= x^2+3x+2x+6$

$\qquad = x^2+5x+6.$

In this part, you can add the like terms $2x$ and $3x$ to get $5x$.

(d) $(x+3)^2 =(x+3)(x+3)$

$\qquad = x^2+3x+3x+9$

$\qquad = x^2+6x+9.$

*Don't be tempted by an **incorrect** shortcut which gives x^2+9.*

As in part (c), you can combine the terms involving x.

The last two examples are very important. Many people do the middle step
mentally, but if you do this, make sure you do it accurately.

Exercise 8B

1 Expand the following pairs of brackets.

(a) $(a+b)(c+d)$ (b) $(p+q)(r-s)$ (c) $(a-b)(c+d)$
(d) $(p-q)(r-s)$ (e) $(a+2)(b+c)$ (f) $(x-y)(x-z)$
(g) $(a+2b)(a-c)$ (h) $(a+4)(a-b)$ (i) $(c+4)(b-4)$

2 Expand the following pairs of brackets and simplify your answers.

(a) $(x+2)(x+1)$ (b) $(x-2)(x+1)$ (c) $(x+2)(x-1)$
(d) $(x-2)(x-1)$ (e) $(3x+1)(2x+3)$ (f) $(x+1)(3x+2)$
(g) $(2x+5)(3x+2)$ (h) $(2x-1)(x-2)$ (i) $(2x+5)(2x-5)$

3 Expand the following pairs of brackets and simplify your answers.

(a) $(x+1)^2$ (b) $(x-1)^2$ (c) $(x-3)^2$
(d) $(x+4)^2$ (e) $(2x+1)^2$ (f) $(2x+3)^2$
(g) $(4x-7)^2$ (h) $(3x-5)^2$ (i) $(2x-1)^2$

8.3 Factorisation by grouping

This section describes the reverse of the process in the previous section.

The next example is given in more detail than the following ones.

Example 8.3.1

Factorise $ax + 2x + 3a + 6$.

$$ax + 2x + 3a + 6 = x(a+2) + 3(a+2)$$
$$= xz + 3z$$
$$= z(x+3)$$
$$= (a+2)(x+3).$$

Split the terms into two groups and factorise each group. Both groups have a factor of $a+2$.

Write $a+2 = z$, and factorise again.

Replace z by $a+2$.

The process can only continue after the first line if the two expressions which appear in the brackets, in this case both $(a+2)$, are the same.

If they are not the same, either your grouping has not worked and you should try another one, or the expression does not factorise.

In doing this kind of working you would usually leave out the middle two lines and write simply

$$ax + 2x + 3a + 6 = x(a+2) + 3(a+2)$$
$$= (a+2)(x+3)$$

with no mention of any intermediate letter z.

In Example 8.3.1, $ax + 3a + 2x + 6$ is another grouping which could be used. This factorises as $a(x+3) + 2(x+3)$, giving $(x+3)(a+2)$ as before.

Example 8.3.2

Factorise the following expressions, if possible.
(a) $ab - ac + 2b - 2c$ (b) $xy + z^2 + yz + xz$
(c) $ab - ac - 3c + 3b$ (d) $pq + qr + pr - p^2$

(a) $ab - ac + 2b - 2c = a(b-c) + 2(b-c)$
$$= (b-c)(a+2).$$

This is similar to Example 8.3.1.

(b) $xy + z^2 + yz + xz = xy + yz + xz + z^2$
$$= y(x+z) + z(x+z)$$
$$= (x+z)(y+z).$$

The original grouping of the terms was unhelpful, so the order was changed.

(c) $ab - ac - 3c + 3b = a(b-c) - 3(c-b)$
$$= a(b-c) + 3(b-c)$$
$$= (b-c)(a+3).$$

The right brackets appear to be different, but as $(c-b) = -(b-c)$, they can be made to be the same.

(d) $pq + qr + pr - p^2 = q(p+r) - p(p-r)$.

$pq + qr + pr - p^2 = pq - p^2 + pr + qr$

$= p(q-p) + r(p+q)$.

The two factors in brackets are not the same, either in the first try or the second. There are no factors.

$pq + qr + pr - p^2$ has no factors.

Factorising expressions of the kind $x^2 + 5x + 6$ is dealt with in Chapter 10.

Exercise 8C

1 Factorise the following expressions.

   (a) $ax + a + x + 1$ (b) $xy + 2x + 2y + 4$ (c) $pq + 4q + 2p + 8$

   (d) $ax + cx + ay + cy$ (e) $ab - 2b + ac - 2c$ (f) $r^2 - 2r + rs - 2s$

   (g) $c^2 - 3c - 3b + bc$ (h) $x^2 - 3y + 3x - xy$ (i) $z^2 + ab - az - bz$

2 Factorise the following expressions, if possible.

   (a) $ax + a + x - 1$ (b) $ax - a + x - 1$ (c) $ax - a - x - 1$

   (d) $-ax - a - x - 1$ (e) $a^2 + ca + ab + c^2$ (f) $r^2 - rs + rs - s^2$

   (g) $p^2 - qr + pq + pr$ (h) $qr - pq - pr + p^2$ (i) $2p^2 + pq - 2pr - qr$

8.4 Some important results to remember

To multiply a pair of brackets, multiply every term in the first bracket by every term in the second, and add the results.

Factorising by grouping works only if each group has the same factor in brackets.

Test exercise 8

1 Factorise the following expressions.

   (a) $ax + 2x$ (b) $pq + p^2$ (c) $2p + 3q + 6 + pq$

   (d) $4z - 3t + 12 - tz$ (e) $2h^2 + 3h - 2hk - 3k$ (f) $ax + ay - az$

2 Expand the following brackets, simplifying your answer where possible.

   (a) $(a+2)(c-2)$ (b) $(2p+1)(p-1)$ (c) $(x-y)(x-2z)$

   (d) $(x+3y)(x-3y)$ (e) $(y-3z)^2$ (f) $(2p+3q)^2$

9 Changing the subject of a formula

Changing the subject of a formula is really about solving equations which contain both letters and numbers. When you have completed this chapter, you should

- be able to solve simple equations to give one letter in terms of the others.

9.1 The subject of a formula

A formula is a mathematical equation containing two or more letters.

Suppose that you have a formula such as $2x = 3a$, where you want to solve the equation to give x in terms of a.

If you divide both sides of the equation by 2, you then get

$$x = \frac{3a}{2} = \frac{3}{2}a.$$

The letter x is then said to be the **subject of the formula**. If you know the value of the other letter, then you can substitute directly to find x.

Similarly, if you divide the equation $2x = 3a$ by 3, you get

$$a = \frac{2x}{3} = \frac{2}{3}x,$$

and a is now the subject of the formula.

9.2 Changing the subject of a formula

Changing the subject of a formula is, except for one step late in the process and which is covered in Section 9.4, exactly the same as solving an equation.

Here are some examples.

Example 9.2.1
In each case, make x the subject of the formula.

(a) $a + x = b + c$ (b) $a + 3x = b + c$ (c) $ax = b + c$ (d) $ax + a = b + c$

(a) $\quad a + x = b + c$	*Get the terms with x on one side,*
$a + x - a = b + c - a$	*and everything else on the other.*
$x = b + c - a.$	*Do this by subtracting a from both sides. (The middle step will be omitted from here on.)*

(b) $a+3x=b+c$ *Subtract a from both sides.*

   $3x=b+c-a$
                                        Divide both sides by 3.
   $x=\frac{1}{3}(b+c-a)$.

(c) $ax=b+c$ *The term with x is already by itself*
                                        on the left, so divide both sides by
   $x=\dfrac{b+c}{a}$.   *a.*

(d) $ax+a=b+c$ *The term with x is not by itself on*
                                        the left, so subtract a from both
   $ax=b+c-a$ *sides.*

   $x=\dfrac{b+c-a}{a}$.
                                        Then divide both sides by a.

Exercise 9A

1 Solve each of the following equations for x.

   (a) $x+a=b$ (b) $x+b=a-b$ (c) $a-x=b$ (d) $a+2x=b$
   (e) $ax=2b$ (f) $ax-b=2b$ (g) $ax+c=b+c$ (h) $ax-b+c=b$

2 In each case, make the letter given at the end the subject of the formula.

   (a) $y=mx+c,\ \ c$ (b) $y=mx+c,\ \ m$ (c) $s=vt,\ \ t$
   (d) $V=IR,\ \ R$ (e) $v^2=u^2+2as,\ \ s$ (f) $v=u+gt,\ \ g$
   (g) $v=u+gt,\ \ u$ (h) $2s=2u+at^2,\ \ a$ (i) $y=a^2x+b^2,\ \ x$

9.3 Formulae with brackets and fractions

If there are brackets in a formula, then, just as with ordinary equations, you should expand them first.

Example 9.3.1

In each case, make x the subject of the formula.

(a) $a(x+b)=c$ (b) $\dfrac{a}{x}=b$ (c) $\dfrac{x}{a}=1+\dfrac{1}{b}$ (d) $\dfrac{x+p}{p}=\dfrac{p}{q}+\dfrac{q}{p}$

   (a) $a(x+b)=c$ *Expand the brackets.*

   $ax+ab=c$
                                        Subtract ab from both sides to get
   $ax=c-ab$ *the term involving x by itself on*
                                        one side.
   $x=\dfrac{c-ab}{a}$.

                                        Divide both sides by a.

(b) $\dfrac{a}{x} = b$

$a = bx$

$bx = a$

$x = \dfrac{a}{b}.$

Multiply both sides by x to get rid of the fraction.

You don't have to swap sides, but most people feel more comfortable with x on the left.

Divide both sides by b.

(c) $\dfrac{x}{a} = 1 + \dfrac{1}{b}$

$\dfrac{xab}{a} = ab + \dfrac{ab}{b}$

$xb = ab + a$

$x = \dfrac{ab + a}{b}.$

To remove the fractions multiply both sides by ab, and cancel. Don't forget to multiply the 1.

You might, as you get confident, leave out this step, as in part (d).

The number multiplying x is b, so divide both sides by b.

(d) $\dfrac{x + p}{p} = \dfrac{p}{q} + \dfrac{q}{p}$

$q(x + p) = p^2 + q^2$

$qx + pq = p^2 + q^2$

$qx = p^2 + q^2 - pq$

$x = \dfrac{p^2 + q^2 - pq}{q}.$

Recall that the fraction bar acts as a bracket, so put the brackets in.

Then multiply both sides by pq, and cancel.

Expand the bracket.

Subtract pq from both sides.

Divide both sides by q.

Exercise 9B

1 Solve each of the following equations for x.

(a) $2(x + a) = b$ (b) $\frac{1}{2}x + 2a = 4b$ (c) $a(x + b) = ab$ (d) $\dfrac{a}{x} = b + c$

(e) $\dfrac{x}{a} = \dfrac{a + b}{b}$ (f) $\dfrac{a(x + b)}{c} = d$ (g) $a(x + c) = c(a + b)$ (h) $\dfrac{x}{a} = \dfrac{a}{b}$

2 In each case, make the letter given at the end the subject of the formula.

(a) $v = \dfrac{d}{t}$, d

(b) $v = \dfrac{d}{t}$, t

(c) $s = ut + \frac{1}{2}at^2$, u

(d) $s = ut + \frac{1}{2}at^2$, a

(e) $\dfrac{v - u}{g} = t$, v

(f) $\dfrac{v - u}{g} = t$, u

(g) $s = \frac{1}{2}t(u + v)$, u

(h) $\dfrac{A - a^2}{a} = 4b$, A

(i) $y = a^2x + b^2$, x

9.4 The need for factorising

When you solve an equation, aim to manipulate it into a form without brackets or fractions, and with all the terms involving the letter you want on one side of the equation, and everything else on the other.

Consider the two parts of the next example, which will be solved side by side.

The solutions are interrupted after the first step by a commentary.

Example 9.4.1
(a) Solve the equation $4x+3=2x+7$.
(b) Make x the subject of the formula $ax+b=cx+d$.

(a) $4x+3=2x+7$ (b) $ax+b=cx+d$

      $4x-2x=7-3$ $ax-cx=d-b$

In part (a) you can continue by doing the calculations on the left and right sides and get the equation $2x=4$; but you can't do that in part (b).

To solve part (b), the important question to ask is 'What multiplies x?' The answer should lead you to factorise the left side.

In both parts the left factorises: $x(4-2)$ and $x(a-c)$.

So, the complete solutions become:

(a) $4x+3=2x+7$ (b) $ax+b=cx+d$

      $4x-2x=7-3$ $ax-cx=d-b$

      $x(4-2)=7-3$ $x(a-c)=d-b$

          $x=\dfrac{7-3}{4-2}=2.$ $x=\dfrac{d-b}{a-c}.$

The processes for the two parts are identical. However, part (a) involves more calculation to complete it.

Example 9.4.2
Make x the subject of the following formulae.

(a) $ax+bx=ab$ (b) $a(x+c)=b(x+c)$ (c) $y=\dfrac{x+a}{x-a}$ (d) $\dfrac{a}{x}+b=c$

(a) $ax+bx=ab$ *The terms with x are already on one*

      $x(a+b)=ab$ *side; everything else is on the other.*

          $x=\dfrac{ab}{a+b}.$ *Factorise the left side, and divide by the factor which multiplies x.*

(b) $a(x+c)=b(x+a)$

Expand the brackets.

$ax+ac=bx+ba$

Add and subtract terms to get the terms with x on one side, and the remaining terms on the other.

$ax-bx=ab-ac$

$x(a-b)=ab-ac$

$x=\dfrac{ab-ac}{a-b}$.

Factorise the left side, and divide by the number which multiplies x.

You might wish to factorise the numerator to get $x=\dfrac{a(b-c)}{a-b}$.

(c) $y=\dfrac{x+a}{x-b}$

Remove the fraction by multiplying by $x-b$. Put in the brackets.

$y(x-b)=x+a$

Expand the brackets.

$yx-yb=x+a$

Add and subtract terms to get the terms with x on one side, and the remaining terms on the other.

$yx-x=a+yb$

$x(y-1)=a+yb$

$x=\dfrac{a+yb}{y-1}$.

Factorise the left side, and divide by the factor which multiplies x.

(d) $\dfrac{a}{x}+b=c$

Remove the fraction by multiplying both sides by x.

$a+bx=cx$

It is more natural, in this case, to collect the x terms on the right.

$a=cx-bx$

$cx-bx=a$

You can swap the sides if you wish.

$x(c-b)=a$

Factorise the left side, and divide by the factor which multiplies x.

$x=\dfrac{a}{c-b}$.

Exercise 9C

1 Solve each of the following equations for x.

(a) $x+xy=y$

(b) $x=y+xy$

(c) $x+y=xy$

(d) $px-qx=p$

(e) $rx+sx-tx=u$

(f) $ax=bx+c$

(g) $hx=k-kx$

(h) $p(x+q)=2q(x+p)$

(i) $ax+b(x-a)=0$

(j) $y=1-\dfrac{1}{x}$

(k) $y=\dfrac{x+1}{x}$

(l) $y=\dfrac{x+1}{x-1}$

(m) $\dfrac{x}{a}=\dfrac{x}{b}-1$

(n) $y=\dfrac{x+k}{x+2k}$

(o) $y=1-\dfrac{1}{x-1}$

2 In each case, make the letter given at the end the subject of the formula.

(a) $A = P + \frac{1}{100} PRT$, T

(b) $A = P + \frac{1}{100} PRT$, P

(c) $s = \frac{1}{2} d(a + l)$, a

(d) $s = \frac{1}{2} d(a + l)$, d

(e) $s = \frac{1}{2} n(2a + d(n-1))$, d

(f) $s = \frac{1}{2}(u + v)t$, t

(g) $\frac{1}{u} + \frac{1}{v} = \frac{1}{f}$, u

(h) $E = \frac{1}{2} mv^2 + mgh$, m

9.5 Roots and powers

Square roots

You know, from Section 6.1, that x^2 is 'x squared' or 'x to the power 2'.

To solve the equation $x^2 = 12$, you need to find the **square root** of 12, written $\sqrt{12}$.

You can find the approximate value of $\sqrt{12}$ using your calculator: it is about 3.464.

Notice that $\sqrt{12}$ is positive, that is, $\sqrt{12} = +3.464$. In fact, the square root of any number is positive, with the exception of 0, where $\sqrt{0} = 0$.

Notice also that $-\sqrt{12}$ also satisfies the equation $x^2 = 12$, since

$$\left(-\sqrt{12}\right) \times \left(-\sqrt{12}\right) = \left(\sqrt{12}\right)^2 = 12.$$

So, if you have the equation $x^2 = a$, then $x = \sqrt{a}$ or $x = -\sqrt{a}$.

Cube roots

Cube roots are less complicated than square roots.

If $x^3 = a$, then x is the cube root of a, written $x = \sqrt[3]{a}$.

There is only one solution to the equation $x^3 = a$.

9.6 Solving equations with roots and powers

The important principle is this: if the letter that you want to solve for, or make the subject of the formula, is squared or cubed, then you have to use the square root or cube root at some stage. If the letter that you want to solve for is having its square root or cube root taken, then at some stage you need to square or cube.

It is not easy to say precisely when you square or cube or square root or cube root. You have to use your judgement.

Example 9.6.1
Solve the following equations for x.

(a) $\sqrt{x} - 1 = a$ (b) $\dfrac{x^2}{a^2} - \dfrac{y^2}{b^2} = 1$ (c) $\sqrt{x+1} = a$

(a) $\sqrt{x} - 1 = a$ *Get $\sqrt{x}$ by itself on the left.*

$\qquad \sqrt{x} = 1 + a$ *Then square both sides.*

$\qquad x = (1+a)^2.$ *Notice the brackets.*

(b) $\qquad \dfrac{x^2}{a^2} - \dfrac{y^2}{b^2} = 1$ *Clear the fractions by multiplying both sides by $a^2 b^2$.*

$\qquad b^2 x^2 - a^2 y^2 = a^2 b^2$

$\qquad b^2 x^2 = a^2 b^2 + a^2 y^2$ *Then solve the equation for x^2.*

$\qquad x^2 = \dfrac{a^2 b^2 + a^2 y^2}{b^2}$ *Finally, take the square root: the sign $\pm$ means 'plus or minus', showing that there are two possible values of x.*

$\qquad x = \pm \sqrt{\dfrac{a^2 b^2 + a^2 y^2}{b^2}}.$

(c) $\sqrt{x+1} = a$ *Start by squaring both sides.*

$\qquad x + 1 = a^2$

$\qquad x = a^2 - 1.$

Exercise 9D

1 Solve each of the following equations for x.

(a) $\sqrt{x} + 1 = a$ (b) $x^2 - 1 = a^2$ (c) $x^2 - y^2 = a^2$

(d) $\sqrt{x^2 + a^2} = a$ (e) $\sqrt[3]{x} - a = 1$ (f) $x^3 - a^3 = 1$

2 In each case, make the letter given at the end the subject of the formula.

(a) $A = 4\pi r^2, \quad r$ (b) $V = \frac{4}{3}\pi r^3, \quad r$ (c) $\dfrac{x^3}{a^3} - \dfrac{y^2}{b^2} = 1, \quad x$

(d) $a y^2 = x^3, \quad y$ (e) $E = \frac{1}{2}mv^2 - \frac{1}{2}mu^2, \quad u$ (f) $V = \pi r^2 h, \quad r$

9.7 Some important results to remember

The technique for changing the subject of a formula is the same as that for solving an equation.

When you have on one side of the equation all the terms involving the letter that you want, and all the remaining terms on the other side, factorise to find the number which multiplies it. Then divide both sides by this number.

Test exercise 9

1 Solve each of the following equations for x.

(a) $ax + bx = x(a - b) + c$

(b) $s = \frac{1}{2}n(x + y)$

(c) $b(x + a) = ab$

(d) $x(b + c) - a = b$

(e) $\frac{x}{a} + \frac{y}{b} = \frac{xy}{ab}$

(f) $\frac{x^3}{a^3} + \frac{y^3}{b^3} = 1$

2 In each case, make the letter given at the end the subject of the formula.

(a) $s = \frac{a}{1 - r}$, r

(b) $A = 2\pi r(r + h)$, h

(c) $\frac{1}{u} + \frac{1}{v} = \frac{1}{f}$, f

(d) $h = \frac{1}{2}gt^2$, t

(e) $v^2 = w^2(a^2 - x^2)$, x

(f) $V = \frac{1}{3}\sqrt{\frac{s^3}{8\pi}}$, s

10 Factorising quadratics

In this chapter you will learn how to factorise expressions of the form $x^2 - 4x - 5$ and $2y^2 - 5y + 2$. When you have completed it you should

- be able to factorise $x^2 - 4x - 5$ as $(x+1)(x-5)$ and $2y^2 - 5y + 2$ as $(y-2)(2y-1)$.

10.1 Expressions like $x^2 - 5x - 14$

In Section 8.2 you learned how to multiply brackets such as $(x+2)(x-7)$.

$$(x+2)(x-7) = x(x-7) + 2(x-7)$$
$$= x^2 - 7x + 2x - 14$$
$$= x^2 - 5x - 14.$$

But, given $x^2 - 5x - 14$, how do you find that $x^2 - 5x - 14 = (x+2)(x-7)$?

Expressions such as $x^2 - 5x - 14$ are called **quadratics**.

Here are some more examples of quadratics.

$$x^2, \quad x^2 + 6x + 8, \quad 2x^2 - 5x + 2, \quad -x^2, \quad 9 - x^2, \quad -9 - 10x - 3x^2, \quad \pi x^2$$

A 'quadratic in x' is any expression which can be written as $ax^2 + bx + c$, where a, b and c are any numbers, not necessarily positive, except that a is not zero.

The number c is called the **constant term**.

So, the quadratic $9 - x^2$, which is the same as $-x^2 + 9$, has $a = -1$, $b = 0$ and $c = 9$.

You can have quadratics in y, such as $2y^2 - 5y + 2$, or in any other letter.

In this chapter, a, b and c are positive or negative whole numbers, and b and c can also be zero.

Exercise 10A

1 In each of the following quadratics $ax^2 + bx + c$ state the values of a, b and c.

  (a) $x^2 + 3x + 5$ (b) $x^2 - x + 7$ (c) $3x^2 + 2x - 1$

  (d) $x^2 - 4$ (e) $1 + 5x^2$ (f) $4 - 2x - x^2$

2 Write down the quadratics $ax^2 + bx + c$ which are given by the following values of a, b and c.

  (a) $a = 1$, $b = -3$, $c = 2$ (b) $a = 2$, $b = 0$, $c = -5$

  (c) $a = -3$, $b = -1$, $c = 4$ (d) $a = 1$, $b = -3$, $c = 0$

10.2 Factorising quadratics of the form $x^2 + bx + c$

There is no easy way to factorise a quadratic. You can get clues by looking at what happens when you multiply out expressions such as $(x+2)(x+3)$.

Look at the signs in the following expansions.

$$(x+2)(x+3) = x^2 + 5x + 6 \qquad\qquad (x-2)(x-3) = x^2 - 5x + 6$$

$$(x-2)(x+3) = x^2 + x - 6 \qquad\qquad (x+2)(x-3) = x^2 - x - 6$$

> If the signs in a quadratic, for example $x^2 + 5x + 6$, are both positive, then the factors are of the form $(x+\dots)(x+\dots)$.
>
> If the sign of the constant term is positive, but the term involving x is negative, for example $x^2 - 5x + 6$, then the factors are of the form $(x-\dots)(x-\dots)$.
>
> If the sign of the constant term is negative, for example $x^2 + x - 6$ or $x^2 - x - 6$, then the factors are of the form $(x-\dots)(x+\dots)$.

Example 10.2.1
Factorise   (a) $x^2 + 6x + 8$,   (b) $y^2 + 8y + 16$.

(a) Both signs are positive, so the factors have the form $(x+\dots)(x+\dots)$.

8 can be factorised as 1×8 and 2×4.

This suggests that you try to factorise as $(x+1)(x+8)$ or $(x+2)(x+4)$.

$(x+1)(x+8) = x^2 + 9x + 8$ and $(x+2)(x+4) = x^2 + 6x + 8$.

So $x^2 + 6x + 8 = (x+2)(x+4)$.

(b) Both signs are positive, so the factors of $y^2 + 8y + 16$ have the form $(y+\dots)(y+\dots)$.

16 can be factorised as 1×16, 2×8 and 4×4.

This suggests that you try to factorise as $(y+1)(y+16), (y+2)(y+8)$ or $(y+4)(y+4)$.

$(y+1)(y+16) = y^2 + 17y + 16$, $(y+2)(y+8) = y^2 + 10y + 16$ and $(y+4)(y+4) = y^2 + 8y + 16$.

So $y^2 + 8y + 16 = (y+4)(y+4)$, which is usually written as $(y+4)^2$.

In practice, you would probably do much of the work in Example 10.2.1 in your head or on rough paper, and all you might write down is the very last line; but for the moment, the examples will show the process in some detail.

The process is the same whatever letter is used for the quadratic. From now on, all the quadratics in the examples will be given in terms of x.

Example 10.2.2
Factorise $x^2 - 3x + 2$.

The factors have the form $(x - \ldots)(x - \ldots)$.

The constant term is 2, which factorises as 1×2.

The only possibility is $(x - 1)(x - 2)$.

Checking, $(x - 1)(x - 2)$ works, so $x^2 - 3x + 2 = (x - 1)(x - 2)$.

You need to check that $(x - 1)(x - 2)$ works, because some quadratics do not have factors. For example, to factorise $x^2 + 3x + 4$, you would try $(x + 1)(x + 4)$ and $(x + 2)(x + 2)$, but neither of them works. The quadratic $x^2 + 3x + 4$ has no factors.

Example 10.2.3
Factorise   (a) $x^2 - 8x + 12$,   (b) $x^2 + 3x - 4$,   (c) $x^2 - 7x - 18$.

(a) $x^2 - 8x + 12$

    The factors have the form $(x - \ldots)(x - \ldots)$.

    12 can be factorised as 1×12, 2×6 and 3×4.

    The possibilities are $(x - 1)(x - 12)$, $(x - 2)(x - 6)$ and $(x - 3)(x - 4)$.

$x^2 - 8x + 12 = (x - 2)(x - 6)$.   *Check which is correct.*

(b) $x^2 + 3x - 4$

    The factors have the form $(x - \ldots)(x + \ldots)$.

    4 can be factorised as 1×4 and 2×2.

    The possibilities are $(x - 1)(x + 4)$, $(x + 1)(x - 4)$ and $(x - 2)(x + 2)$.

$x^2 + 3x - 4 = (x - 1)(x + 4)$.   *Check which is correct.*

(c) $x^2 - 7x - 18$

    The factors have the form $(x - \ldots)(x + \ldots)$.

    18 can be factorised as 1×18, 2×9 and 3×6.

    The possibilities are
$$(x - 1)(x + 18) \qquad (x - 18)(x + 1)$$
$$(x - 2)(x + 9) \qquad (x - 9)(x + 2)$$
$$(x - 3)(x + 6) \qquad (x - 6)(x + 3).$$

$x^2 - 7x - 18 = (x - 9)(x + 2)$.   *Check which is correct.*

Example 10.2.4
Show that $x^2 + 1$ has no factors.

The only possibility is $(x+1)(x+1)$, but $(x+1)(x+1) = x^2 + 2x + 1$, so $x^2 + 1$ has no factors.

Exercise 10B

1 Factorise each of the following quadratics.
(a) $x^2 + 3x + 2$ (b) $x^2 + 4x + 3$ (c) $x^2 + 4x + 4$
(d) $y^2 + 9y + 8$ (e) $x^2 + 7x + 10$ (f) $x^2 + 6x + 9$
(g) $x^2 + 11x + 24$ (h) $p^2 + 9p + 20$ (i) $x^2 + 9x + 18$
(j) $k^2 + 22k + 21$ (k) $x^2 + 11x + 30$ (l) $x^2 + 19x + 60$

2 Factorise each of the following quadratics.
(a) $x^2 - 4x + 3$ (b) $a^2 - 5a + 4$ (c) $x^2 - 7x + 6$
(d) $x^2 - 9x + 8$ (e) $x^2 - 2x + 1$ (f) $l^2 - 7l + 12$
(g) $z^2 - 13z + 22$ (h) $x^2 - 10x + 25$ (i) $x^2 - 11x + 28$
(j) $x^2 - 12x + 32$ (k) $q^2 - 12q + 35$ (l) $x^2 - 16x + 60$

3 Factorise each of the following quadratics.
(a) $x^2 + x - 2$ (b) $x^2 - x - 2$ (c) $c^2 - 3c - 4$
(d) $x^2 + x - 6$ (e) $d^2 - 2d - 8$ (f) $x^2 + 7x - 8$
(g) $h^2 + 9h - 22$ (h) $x^2 - x - 12$ (i) $x^2 + 5x - 24$
(j) $x^2 - 3x - 18$ (k) $x^2 + 10x - 56$ (l) $n^2 - 7n - 60$

4 Factorise the quadratics which have factors, and write 'no factors' for the others.
(a) $s^2 - 3s - 4$ (b) $x^2 - 13x + 40$ (c) $x^2 - 12x + 40$
(d) $x^2 - 3x - 10$ (e) $x^2 + 6x - 12$ (f) $t^2 + 8t + 15$
(g) $x^2 - 8x - 9$ (h) $m^2 - 3m + 3$ (i) $x^2 + 10x + 9$
(j) $x^2 + 9x + 14$ (k) $x^2 - 10x - 15$ (l) $y^2 + 10y + 25$
(m) $r^2 - 17r + 32$ (n) $x^2 + 4x - 21$ (o) $x^2 - 14x + 33$
(p) $x^2 + 16x + 12$ (q) $j^2 - 4j - 60$ (r) $x^2 + 11x - 60$
(s) $x^2 - 2$ (t) $x^2 - 4$ (u) x^2

10.3 Factorising quadratics of the form $ax^2 + bx + c$

In Section 10.2 you factorised quadratics of the form $ax^2 + bx + c$ where a was equal to 1.

The same principles and the same rules about signs still work when a is not 1.

Look at the signs in the following expansions.

$$(2x+3)(5x+7)=10x^2+29x+21 \qquad (2x-3)(5x-7)=10x^2-29x+21$$

$$(2x-3)(5x+7)=10x^2-x-21 \qquad (2x+3)(5x-7)=10x^2+x-21$$

You can see that the rules about signs have not changed.

Example 10.3.1

Factorise   (a) $2x^2-7x+3$,   (b) $7x^2-2x-5$,   (c) $6x^2-x-2$.

(a) $2x^2-7x+3$

The factors of $2x^2$ are $2x \times x$.

The factors of 3 are $3=3\times1$.

The possibilities are $(x-1)(2x-3)$ and $(x-3)(2x-1)$.

$2x^2-7x+3=(x-3)(2x-1)$.   *Check which is correct.*

(b) $7x^2-2x-5$

The factors of $7x^2$ are $7x \times x$.

The factors of 5 are 5×1.

The possibilities are

$$(7x-1)(x+5) \qquad (7x+1)(x-5)$$
$$(x-1)(7x+5) \qquad (x+1)(7x-5).$$

$7x^2-2x-5=(x-1)(7x+5)$.   *Check which is correct.*

(c) $6x^2-x-2$

The factors of $6x^2$ are $2x \times 3x$ or $x \times 6x$.

The factors of 2 are 2×1.

The possibilities are

$$(x-1)(6x+2) \qquad (x+1)(6x-2)$$
$$(2x-1)(3x+2) \qquad (2x+1)(3x-2)$$
$$(3x-1)(2x+2) \qquad (3x+1)(2x-2)$$
$$(6x-1)(x+2) \qquad (6x+1)(x-2)$$

$6x^2-x-2=(2x+1)(3x-2)$.   *Check which is correct.*

Factorising gets very hard because the number of possible pairs of factors can be large. Don't spend too long if you cannot see factors of this type of quadratic very quickly.

There are methods which you can use for factorising quadratics when the numbers become big, but they are not covered in this book.

Example 10.3.2

Express $2x^2 + 8x - 10$ as a product of factors.

$2x^2 + 8x - 10$

> *You can save yourself time by seeing that 2 divides the quadratic, and factorising it first as $2(x^2 + 4x - 5)$.*
>
> *Then, factorise the quadratic $x^2 + 4x - 5$ as $(x-1)(x+5)$.*

$2x^2 + 8x - 10 = 2(x - 1)(x + 5).$

Sometimes, when a is negative, quadratics are written with the x^2 term at the end. Finding the factors of quadratics written this way, such as $5 - 3x - 2x^2$, involves no new principles.

Example 10.3.3

Find the factors of $5 - 3x - 2x^2$.

$5 - 3x - 2x^2$

> *The possibilities are*
>
> $(1 - x)(5 + 2x)$ $(1 + x)(5 - 2x)$
> $(1 - 2x)(5 + x)$ $(1 + 2x)(5 - x).$

$5 - 3x - 2x^2 = (1 - x)(5 + 2x).$

> *Check which is correct.*

Exercise 10C

1 Factorise each of the following quadratics.

(a) $2x^2 + 3x + 1$ (b) $2x^2 - 5x + 2$ (c) $3x^2 + 5x + 2$

(d) $2x^2 - 7x + 5$ (e) $3x^2 - 8x + 4$ (f) $6x^2 + 5x + 1$

(g) $9x^2 - 6x + 1$ (h) $9x^2 + 12x + 4$ (i) $4x^2 - 12x + 5$

(j) $6x^2 - 13x + 6$ (k) $3x^2 + 14x + 8$ (l) $60x^2 + 19x + 1$

2 Factorise each of the following quadratics.

(a) $2x^2 - x - 1$ (b) $3x^2 + 2x - 1$ (c) $6x^2 - x - 1$

(d) $12x^2 + x - 1$ (e) $2x^2 + 3x - 2$ (f) $2x^2 - x - 3$

(g) $4x^2 - 7x - 2$ (h) $3x^2 - 4x - 4$ (i) $8x^2 - 15x - 2$

(j) $6x^2 + 5x - 6$ (k) $4x^2 - 8x - 5$ (l) $6x^2 - 11x - 10$

3 Factorise the following quadratics completely by first taking out the common factor.

(a) $2x^2 + 2x - 4$ (b) $4x^2 + 16x + 16$ (c) $9x^2 - 30x + 9$

(d) $4x^2 + 8x - 12$ (e) $6x^2 + 36x + 54$ (f) $8x^2 - 24x + 10$

(g) $12x^2 - 10x - 8$ (h) $4x^2 + 14x + 10$ (i) $18x^2 + 24x + 8$

4 Factorise each of the following quadratics.

(a) $2 + 3x + x^2$

(b) $2 + 3x - 2x^2$

(c) $4 + 3x - x^2$

(d) $6 - 5x - x^2$

(e) $10 + 3x - x^2$

(f) $2 + x - 3x^2$

(g) $4 + 5x - 6x^2$

(h) $8 - 2x - 15x^2$

(i) $6 + x - 12x^2$

10.4 The difference of two squares

The difference of two squares refers to quadratics like $x^2 - 9$ and $81 - 4x^2$, where there is no term involving x, and both the other terms are squares separated by a minus sign.

Example 10.4.1

Factorise $x^2 - 9$.

$$x^2 - 9$$

The possibilities are $(x-1)(x+9)$, $(x+1)(x-9)$ and $(x+3)(x-3)$.

$$x^2 - 9 = (x + 3)(x - 3).$$

Check which is correct.

Notice that

$$(x + k)(x - k) = x(x - k) + k(x - k)$$
$$= x^2 - kx + kx - k^2$$
$$= x^2 - k^2.$$

You can generalise the result of Example 10.4.1 to:

> **Difference of two squares rule:**
>
> $$x^2 - k^2 = (x + k)(x - k)$$

Example 10.4.2

Factorise   (a) $x^2 - 4$,   (b) $9x^2 - 16$,   (c) $81 - 4x^2$,   (d) $16x^2 - y^2$.

(a) $x^2 - 4 = (x + 2)(x - 2)$.

Use $x^2 - k^2 = (x + k)(x - k)$ with $k = 2$.

(b) $9x^2 - 16 = (3x + 4)(3x - 4)$.

$9x^2 - 16$ is $(3x)^2 - 4^2$. Apply the difference of two squares rule.

(c) $81 - 4x^2 = (9 + 2x)(9 - 2x)$.

$81 - 4x^2 = 9^2 - (2x)^2$. Apply the difference of two squares rule.

(d) $16x^2 - y^2 = (4x + y)(4x - y)$.

$16x^2 - y^2 = (4x)^2 - y^2$. Apply the difference of two squares rule.

Sometimes the difference of two squares method of factorising can be used to save multiplying out brackets. Here is an example.

Example 10.4.3
Factorise $(3y+1)^2 - (y+2)^2$.

$$(3y+1)^2 - (y+2)^2$$
$$= \{(3y+1)+(y+2)\}\{(3y+1)-(y+2)\}$$
$$= \{3y+1+y+2\}\{3y+1-y-2\}$$
$$= (4y+3)(2y-1).$$

Use $x^2 - k^2 = (x+k)(x-k)$
with $x = 3y+1$ *and* $k = y+2$.

Then expand the inside brackets.

Finally simplify the brackets.

It is left to you to check that this is the same result that you get if you start by expanding $(3y+1)^2$ and $(y+2)^2$.

Exercise 10D

1 Find the factors of each of the following quadratics.

(a) $x^2 - 1$ (b) $x^2 - 81$ (c) $4x^2 - 9$

(d) $9x^2 - 1$ (e) $4 - 25d^2$ (f) $8z^2 - 32$

2 Find the factors of each of the following quadratics.

(a) $3x^2 - 27$ (b) $50 - 2y^2$ (c) $100 - 4z^2$

(d) $(x+1)^2 - 4x^2$ (e) $(2x+1)^2 - x^2$ (f) $(2x+1)^2 - (x-3)^2$

10.5 Some important results to remember

The form $ax^2 + bx$

These are easy to factorise and do not require the methods of this chapter. Simply take out the common factor of x. So $ax^2 + bx = x(ax+b)$.

The general quadratic $ax^2 + bx + c$

Not all quadratics factorise. The methods of this chapter show you how to factorise simple quadratics.

The difference of two squares $x^2 - k^2$

These factorise into two similar looking brackets with different signs.
$x^2 - k^2 = (x+k)(x-k)$.

The sum of two squares $x^2 + k^2$

Examples of the sum of two squares are $x^2 + 9$ and $81 + 4x^2$.
Although the sum of two squares may appear similar to the difference, don't be misled. The sum of two squares does not factorise.

Test exercise 10

1 Factorise, where possible, each of the following quadratics.

(a) $3x^2 + 2x$ (b) $1 + 4x + 3x^2$ (c) $9 - 25y^2$

(d) $3p^2 + 4p - 4$ (e) $3x^2 - 15x + 12$ (f) $6s^2 + 54$

(g) $4x - 5x^2$ (h) $4a^2 - 20a + 25$ (i) $2 - 2w^2$

(j) $12x^2 + x - 6$ (k) $3 + 5x - 4x^2$ (l) $8t^2 + 16t - 10$

(m) $12 - 36x + 27x^2$ (n) $2 + 4x^2$ (o) $42 + 8x - 2x^2$

11 Quadratic equations

In this chapter you will learn how to solve quadratic equations like $x^2 - 3x + 2 = 0$. When you have completed it you should

- know that not all quadratic equations have solutions
- be able to solve quadratic equations by factorising
- be able to solve quadratic equations using the formula $x = \dfrac{-b \pm \sqrt{b^2 - 4ac}}{2a}$.

11.1 What is a quadratic equation?

The equations which you met in Chapter 3 which ended up being of the form $ax = b$ are called **linear equations**.

An equation of the form $ax^2 + bx + c = 0$, where a, b and c are constants, is called a **quadratic equation**.

Examples of quadratic equations are

$$x^2 - 3x + 2 = 0, \quad x^2 - 4 = 0, \quad 3x^2 + 2x - 4 = 0, \quad x^2 = 0.$$

The first step in solving a quadratic equation is to collect all the terms on one side of the equation, and to make the number which multiplies x^2 positive.

11.2 Solution by factorising

The simplest way to solve a quadratic equation is to start by factorising the quadratic.

You should know from Chapter 10 that not all quadratics factorise. However, if the quadratic does factorise easily, use this method to solve the equation.

The idea behind the solution is that if two numbers multiply to give the number 0, then one or the other (or both) must be 0.

Example 11.2.1
Solve the quadratic equation $x^2 - 3x + 2 = 0$.

$$x^2 - 3x + 2 = 0$$
$$(x-1)(x-2) = 0$$
Either $(x-1) = 0$ or $(x-2) = 0$.
If $x - 1 = 0$ then $x = 1$.
If $x - 2 = 0$ then $x = 2$.
Either $x = 1$ or $x = 2$.

Factorise the quadratic $x^2 - 3x + 2$.

If two numbers multiply to give 0, then one or the other must be 0.

Consider the possibilities in turn.

There are two possible values for x.

It is characteristic of quadratic equations that the solution consists of two values of x, but you will see later in the chapter that this is not always the case.

The individual values, $x = 1$ and $x = 2$, are called the **roots** of the equation.

Example 11.2.2
Solve the quadratic equations

(a) $2x^2 - 5x + 2 = 0$,   (b) $2x^2 - 5x = 0$,   (c) $3x^2 = 10x - 3$,   (d) $x^2 - 9 = 0$.

(a) $2x^2 - 5x + 2 = 0$ *Factorise the quadratic $2x^2 - 5x + 2$.*

$(2x - 1)(x - 2) = 0$ *If two numbers multiply to give 0, then one or the other must be 0.*

Either $(2x - 1) = 0$ or $(x - 2) = 0$.

If $2x - 1 = 0$ then $2x = 1$ so $x = \frac{1}{2}$.   *Consider the possibilities in turn.*

If $x - 2 = 0$ then $x = 2$.   *There are two roots of the equation,*

Either $x = \frac{1}{2}$ or $x = 2$. $x = \frac{1}{2}$ *and $x = 2$.*

(b) $2x^2 - 5x = 0$ *Factorise the quadratic $2x^2 - 5x$.*

$x(2x - 5) = 0$

Either $x = 0$ or $(2x - 5) = 0$.   *Consider the possibilities in turn. One of them doesn't need much thought.*

If $2x - 5 = 0$ then $x = \frac{5}{2}$.

Either $x = 0$ or $x = \frac{5}{2}$.   *The two roots are $x = 0$ and $x = 2\frac{1}{2}$.*

(c) $3x^2 = 10x - 3$ *Start by collecting all the terms on the left side.*

$3x^2 - 10x + 3 = 0$

$(3x - 1)(x - 3) = 0$ *Factorise the quadratic $3x^2 - 10x + 3$.*

Either $(3x - 1) = 0$ or $(x - 3) = 0$.   *Consider the possibilities in turn.*

If $3x - 1 = 0$ then $x = \frac{1}{3}$.

If $x - 3 = 0$ then $x = 3$.

Either $x = \frac{1}{3}$ or $x = 3$.   *The two roots are $x = \frac{1}{3}$ and $x = 3$.*

(d) $x^2 - 9 = 0$ *Factorise the quadratic $x^2 - 9$, using the difference of two squares.*

$(x + 3)(x - 3) = 0$

Either $(x + 3) = 0$ or $(x - 3) = 0$.   *Consider the possibilities in turn.*

If $x + 3 = 0$ then $x = -3$.

If $x - 3 = 0$ then $x = 3$.

Either $x = -3$ or $x = 3$.   *The two roots are $x = -3$ and $x = 3$.*

You could also solve the last equation by writing it as $x^2 = 9$, giving $x = \pm\sqrt{9} = \pm 3$.

Example 11.2.3
Solve the quadratic equation $x^2 - 8x + 16 = 0$.

$x^2 - 8x + 16 = 0$	*Factorise the quadratic.*
$(x-4)(x-4) = 0$	*The two brackets are the same, so*
Either $(x-4) = 0$ or $(x-4) = 0$.	*when you consider the possibilities*
In both cases $x - 4 = 0$ so $x = 4$.	*in turn there is only one solution.*
The solution is $x = 4$.	*The root is $x = 4$.*

When the two roots are equal, the equation is said to have a **repeated root**. In Example 11.2.3 the equation $x^2 - 8x + 16 = 0$ has a repeated root at $x = 4$.

Exercise 11A

1 Rearrange the following quadratic equations into the form $ax^2 + bx + c = 0$, where a is positive. You do not need to solve the equations.

(a) $x^2 + 2x = 5$ (b) $2x^2 - 10 = x$ (c) $3 + 4x = x^2$

(d) $x(x-4) = 3$ (e) $x(2-3x) = -1$ (f) $2x + 5 = 7x(x-1)$

2 Solve the following quadratic equations.

(a) $x^2 + 3x + 2 = 0$ (b) $x^2 - 4x + 3 = 0$ (c) $x^2 - 4x + 4 = 0$

(d) $c^2 - 3c - 4 = 0$ (e) $x^2 + 9x + 20 = 0$ (f) $t^2 - 12t + 35 = 0$

(g) $d^2 = 15 - 2d$ (h) $x^2 + 11x + 30 = 0$ (i) $56 = x^2 + 10x$

(j) $x^2 - 12x + 32 = 0$ (k) $y^2 + 10y + 25 = 0$ (l) $12 + x = x^2$

3 Find the roots of the following equations.

(a) $x^2 + 3x = 0$ (b) $x^2 - 4x = 0$ (c) $4 - x^2 = 0$

(d) $x^2 - 25 = 0$ (e) $4x^2 + 25x = 0$ (f) $4x^2 - 25 = 0$

4 Find the roots of the following equations.

(a) $2x^2 - x - 1 = 0$ (b) $6 + x - 12x^2 = 0$ (c) $6x^2 - 5x - 4 = 0$

(d) $4x^2 - 7x - 2 = 0$ (e) $6x^2 = 11x + 10$ (f) $8x^2 - 24x + 10 = 0$

11.3 The quadratic equation formula

The factorising method for solving quadratic equations works well if the solutions are whole numbers or easy fractions.

However, the factorising method becomes hopelessly difficult if the solutions involve square roots, if there are no solutions, or if the quadratic is so complicated that you can't factorise it.

In that case, you need the quadratic equation formula.

$$\text{The roots of the equation } ax^2 + bx + c = 0 \text{ are } x = \frac{-b \pm \sqrt{b^2 - 4ac}}{2a}.$$

No proof of this formula is given in this book.

When you use the formula, remember that the fraction bar, acting as a bracket, goes under the whole of the top line.

The first example is easier to solve by factorising, but is there to show how the formula works.

Example 11.3.1
Use the quadratic equation formula to solve the following quadratic equations.

(a) $x^2 + 3x + 2 = 0$ (b) $4x^2 = 7x + 2$ (c) $6 - x^2 = x$

(a) $x^2 + 3x + 2 = 0$

$$x = \frac{-3 \pm \sqrt{3^2 - 4 \times 1 \times 2}}{2 \times 1}$$

$$= \frac{-3 \pm \sqrt{9 - 8}}{2}$$

$$= \frac{-3 \pm \sqrt{1}}{2}$$

$$= \frac{-3 \pm 1}{2}.$$

Either $x = \frac{-3+1}{2} = -1$ or $x = \frac{-3-1}{2} = -2.$

For this equation,
$a = 1, b = 3$ and $c = 2$.

Substitute these values into the quadratic equation formula.

Follow the formula through carefully.

This quadratic factorises, giving $(x+2)(x+1)=0$, so $x = -2$ or $x = -1$, which agrees with the formula.

(b) $4x^2 = 7x + 2$

$$4x^2 - 7x - 2 = 0$$

$$x = \frac{-(-7) \pm \sqrt{(-7)^2 - 4 \times 4 \times (-2)}}{2 \times 4}$$

$$= \frac{7 \pm \sqrt{49 + 32}}{8}$$

$$= \frac{7 \pm \sqrt{81}}{8}$$

$$= \frac{7 \pm 9}{8}.$$

Either $x = \frac{7+9}{8} = 2$ or $x = \frac{7-9}{8} = -\frac{1}{4}.$

Collect the terms on the left.

For this equation,
$a = 4, b = -7$ and $c = -2$.

Substitute these values into the quadratic equation formula.

Follow the formula through carefully, paying special attention to the signs. That is, $-(-7) = 7$ and $(-7)^2 = +49$.

This quadratic factorises, giving $(x-2)(4x+1)=0$, so $x = 2$ or $x = -\frac{1}{4}$, agreeing with the formula.

(c) $6-x^2=x$

$$x^2+x-6=0$$

$$x=\frac{-1\pm\sqrt{1^2-4\times1\times(-6)}}{2\times1}$$

$$=\frac{-1\pm\sqrt{1+24}}{2}$$

$$=\frac{-1\pm\sqrt{25}}{2}=\frac{-1\pm5}{2}.$$

Either $x=\frac{-1+5}{2}=2$ or $x=\frac{-1-5}{2}=-3$.

First rearrange this equation in the form in which you can compare it with $ax^2+bx+c=0$.

For this equation, $a=1, b=1$ and $c=-6$.

Substitute these values into the quadratic equation formula.

This quadratic also factorises, giving $(x+3)(x-2)=0$.

In all the examples, note how much care was taken to keep the signs correct.

Example 11.3.2

Use the quadratic equation formula to solve the following quadratic equations. Give your answers correct to 3 significant figures.

(a) $2x^2+4x+1=0$ (b) $4x^2-7x-3=0$

(a) $2x^2+4x+1=0$

$$x=\frac{-4\pm\sqrt{4^2-4\times2\times1}}{2\times2}=\frac{-4\pm\sqrt{16-8}}{4}$$

$$=\frac{-4\pm\sqrt{8}}{4}=\frac{-4\pm2.828...}{4}.$$

Either $x=\frac{-4+2.8284...}{4}=\frac{-1.1715...}{4}=-0.2928...$

or $x=\frac{-4-2.8284...}{4}=\frac{-6.8284...}{4}=-1.7071....$

So $x=-0.293$ or -1.71, correct to 3 significant figures.

Substitute $a=2$, $b=4$ and $c=1$ in the formula.

Use a calculator for the square root.

Only the first four decimal places are shown, but all the figures have been used.

(b) $4x^2-7x-3=0$

$$x=\frac{-(-7)\pm\sqrt{(-7)^2-4\times4\times(-3)}}{2\times4}$$

$$=\frac{7\pm\sqrt{49+48}}{8}=\frac{7\pm\sqrt{97}}{8}=\frac{7\pm9.8488...}{8}.$$

Either $x=\frac{7+9.8488...}{8}=\frac{16.8488...}{8}=2.1061...$

or $x=\frac{7-9.8488...}{8}=\frac{-2.8488...}{8}=-0.3561...$

$x=2.11$ or -0.356, correct to 3 significant figures.

Substitute $a=4$, $b=-7$ and $c=-3$ in the formula.

Use a calculator for the square root.

Only the first four decimal places are shown.

The formula can also reveal when a quadratic equation has no roots.

If there are no roots, the quadratic formula will end with a negative number under the square root sign.

Here is an example.

Example 11.3.3
Show that the equation $4x^2 + 20x + 27 = 0$ has no roots.

$$4x^2 + 20x + 27 = 0$$

Substitute $a = 4, b = 20$ *and* $c = 27$ *in the formula.*

$$x = \frac{-20 \pm \sqrt{20^2 - 4 \times 4 \times 27}}{2 \times 4}$$

$$= \frac{-20 \pm \sqrt{400 - 432}}{8} = \frac{-4 \pm \sqrt{-32}}{8}.$$

As negative numbers do not have square roots, the quadratic equation has no solution.

If the value of $b^2 - 4ac$ is negative the quadratic equation has no roots.

Exercise 11B

1   Use the quadratic equation formula to solve the following quadratic equations, which all have solutions that are whole numbers or fractions.

    (a) $x^2 + 7x + 10 = 0$ (b) $x^2 - 9x + 20 = 0$ (c) $x^2 - 3x - 18 = 0$

    (d) $2x^2 - 7x + 5 = 0$ (e) $3p^2 + 4p - 4 = 0$ (f) $3 + 4q - 4q^2 = 0$

    (g) $9x^2 - 24x + 16 = 0$ (h) $x^2 = 6x + 27$ (i) $3x^2 = 16 - 13x$

2   Use the quadratic equation formula to solve the following quadratic equations, giving your answers correct to 3 significant figures.

    (a) $x^2 + 7x + 9 = 0$ (b) $x^2 - 9x + 9 = 0$ (c) $x^2 = 3x + 5$

    (d) $2x^2 - 8x - 5 = 0$ (e) $3y^2 + 4y - 6 = 0$ (f) $3x^2 - 2x - 7 = 0$

    (g) $5x^2 = 6 + 3x$ (h) $6 + 3x = 8x^2$ (i) $4x^2 - x - 7 = 0$

3   Not all the following quadratic equations have roots. If they do, find them, giving your answers correct to 3 significant figures where appropriate. If they have no roots, say so. Use whatever method seems best.

    (a) $x^2 - 2x - 5 = 0$ (b) $2x^2 = 4x + 7$ (c) $x^2 - 3x + 18 = 0$

    (d) $3x^2 - 19x + 6 = 0$ (e) $3p^2 + 4p + 4 = 0$ (f) $0.1x^2 + 10x = 1$

    (g) $3x^2 - 10x + 6 = 0$ (h) $x^2 = \sqrt{5}x + 1$ (i) $3x^2 = 13x - 16$

11.4 An important result to remember

The quadratic equation $ax^2 + bx + c = 0$ has roots

$$x = \frac{-b \pm \sqrt{b^2 - 4ac}}{2a}.$$

When $b^2 - 4ac$ is negative, the equation $ax^2 + bx + c = 0$ has no roots.

Test exercise 11

1 Find the roots, if any, of the following quadratic equations. Where appropriate give your answers correct to 3 significant figures.

(a) $2x^2 - 7x + 3 = 0$ (b) $2x^2 - 7x - 4 = 0$ (c) $2x^2 - 4x - 7 = 0$

(d) $3x^2 + 4x + 5 = 0$ (e) $4x^2 - 5x - 6 = 0$ (f) $x^2 + x - 1 = 0$

12 Simultaneous equations

This chapter is about solving pairs of simultaneous equations. When you have completed it, you should

- be able to solve pairs of equations like $\left.\begin{array}{r} x+2y= \ \ 7 \\ 2x-3y=-7 \end{array}\right\}$.

12.1 Adding and subtracting equations

Suppose that you have a very simple pair of equations like

$$\left.\begin{array}{r} a=b \\ c=d \end{array}\right\}.$$

Then it is easy to deduce that

$$a+c=b+d \quad \text{and} \quad a-c=b-d.$$

This process will be called **adding** or **subtracting** the equations.

Similarly, you know that you can multiply an equation by a number; for example, if $c=d$, then multiplying by 3 gives $3c=3d$. So it is easy to see that you can add or subtract multiples of equations:

$$a+3c=b+3d \quad \text{and} \quad a-5c=b-5d.$$

You can also deduce that

$$3a+5c=3b+5d \quad \text{and} \quad 3a-5c=3b-5d.$$

It is clear that you can substitute any other numbers for the 3 and the 5 in the algebraic statements above.

You can apply these ideas to solving the equations $\left.\begin{array}{r} x+2y= \ \ 7 \\ 2x-3y=-7 \end{array}\right\}$ above.

Pairs of equations like $\left.\begin{array}{r} x+2y= \ \ 7 \\ 2x-3y=-7 \end{array}\right\}$ are called **simultaneous** equations.

Simultaneous equations each have two unknown letters, in this case x and y. Solving them means finding the values of x and y which satisfy both the equations at the same time.

The method will be to add and subtract multiples of the equations until you get an equation which you can solve by methods you already know.

Example 12.1.1

Add the equations $\begin{aligned} x-2y&=3\\ 3x+2y&=5 \end{aligned}\Big\}$.

$$\begin{aligned} x-2y&=3\\ 3x+2y&=5 \end{aligned}\Big\}$$

$$4x \quad\ = 8.$$

Most people add down in columns as in this case.

Adding $-2y$ to $+2y$ gives 0.

Subtracting equations needs a little more care with signs.

For example, suppose that you were subtracting $3x-2y=6$ from $3x+y=9$.

The result would be

$$(3x+y)-(3x-2y)=9-6,$$

which gives

$$3x+y-3x+2y=3, \text{ which is } 3y=3.$$

Usually you will want to subtract with a layout like that of Example 12.1.1.

Example 12.1.2

In each case subtract the second equation from the first.

(a) $\begin{aligned} 3x+2y&=7\\ x+2y&=3 \end{aligned}\Big\}$ (b) $\begin{aligned} 3x-2y&=7\\ -x-2y&=3 \end{aligned}\Big\}$

(a) $\begin{aligned} 3x+2y&=7\\ x+2y&=3 \end{aligned}\Big\}$

$$2x \quad\ = 4.$$

There are no difficulties in this case.

(b) $\begin{aligned} 3x-2y&=7\\ -x-2y&=3 \end{aligned}\Big\}$

$$4x \quad\ = 4.$$

In this case, you must remember that subtracting $-x$ is the same as adding x, that is $3x-(-x)=4x$.

Exercise 12A

Keep your answers for use in Exercise 12B.

1 Add the following equations. (You do not need to solve the equations at this stage.)

(a) $\begin{aligned} 2x+3y&=7\\ 4x-3y&=5 \end{aligned}\Big\}$ (b) $\begin{aligned} 5x-y&=4\\ -3x+y&=4 \end{aligned}\Big\}$ (c) $\begin{aligned} -x+y&=5\\ -4x-y&=5 \end{aligned}\Big\}$

(d) $\begin{aligned} -3x+\ y&=3\\ 3x+4y&=7 \end{aligned}\Big\}$ (e) $\begin{aligned} x-3y&=5\\ -x-4y&=9 \end{aligned}\Big\}$ (f) $\begin{aligned} x+3y&=15\\ -x-4y&=-9 \end{aligned}\Big\}$

2   In each part, subtract the second equation from the first. (You do not need to solve the equations at this stage.)

(a) $\begin{aligned}2x+3y&=7\\x+3y&=5\end{aligned}\Big\}$

(b) $\begin{aligned}5x-y&=4\\-3x-y&=4\end{aligned}\Big\}$

(c) $\begin{aligned}-x-2y&=3\\-3x-2y&=5\end{aligned}\Big\}$

(d) $\begin{aligned}3x+5y&=3\\3x+4y&=-3\end{aligned}\Big\}$

(e) $\begin{aligned}-x-3y&=5\\-x-4y&=9\end{aligned}\Big\}$

(f) $\begin{aligned}-2x+3y&=15\\-2x-4y&=-6\end{aligned}\Big\}$

12.2 Solving simultaneous equations

You have probably spotted how to proceed with the sets of equations in Exercise 12A.

In each case, you can reduce the equations to one involving x alone, or one involving y alone. This is called **eliminating** x or y.

You can always do this if the numbers multiplying one of the unknown letters either are the same or differ only in sign.

This is the case for y in the three parts of Example 12.2.1.

You then have to decide whether to add or subtract to eliminate the letter.

Example 12.2.1
Solve the following simultaneous equations.

(a) $\begin{aligned}x-2y&=3\\3x+2y&=5\end{aligned}\Big\}$

(b) $\begin{aligned}3x+2y&=7\\x+2y&=3\end{aligned}\Big\}$

(c) $\begin{aligned}3x-2y&=7\\-x-2y&=3\end{aligned}\Big\}$

(a) $\begin{aligned}x-2y&=3 &&①\\3x+2y&=5 &&②\end{aligned}\Big\}$

$4x \quad\quad = 8 \quad\quad ③$

$x = 2.$

It is good practice to label the equations.

Add Equations ① and ② to eliminate y. Call the new equation Equation ③.

Then solve Equation ③ for x.

$2 - 2y = 3$

$-2y = 1$

$y = -\frac{1}{2}.$

Substitute this value of x in the simpler of the original equations, in this case Equation ①.

Solve this equation to find y.

The solution is $x = 2, y = -\frac{1}{2}$.

Check the solution in the other equation, Equation ②.

$3 \times 2 + 2 \times \left(-\frac{1}{2}\right) = 6 - 1 = 5 \checkmark$

(b) $\left.\begin{array}{l}3x+2y=7 \\ x+2y=3\end{array}\right\}$ ① ②

$2x \quad\quad = 4$ ③

$x = 2.$

$2+2y=3$

$2y=1$

$y = \frac{1}{2}.$

The solution is $x=2, y=\frac{1}{2}$.

Subtract Equation ② from Equation ① to eliminate y.

Then solve Equation ③ for x.

Substitute this value of x in the simpler of the original equations, in this case Equation ②.

Solve this equation to find y.

Check the solution in the other equation, Equation ③.
$3\times2+2\times\frac{1}{2}=6+1=7$ ✓

(c) $\left.\begin{array}{l}3x-2y=7 \\ -x-2y=3\end{array}\right\}$ ① ②

$4x \quad\quad = 4$ ③

$x = 1.$

$-1-2y=3$

$-2y=4$

$y=-2.$

The solution is $x=1, y=-2$.

Subtract Equation ② from Equation ① to eliminate y.

Then solve Equation ③ for x.

Substitute this value of x in the simpler of the original equations, in this case Equation ②.

Solve this equation to find y.

Check the solution in the other equation, Equation ③.
$3\times1-2\times(-2)=3+4=7$ ✓

Exercise 12B

In this exercise, use the answers which you kept from Exercise 12A.

1 Solve the following simultaneous equations.

(a) $\left.\begin{array}{l}2x+3y=7 \\ 4x-3y=5\end{array}\right\}$

(b) $\left.\begin{array}{l}5x-y=4 \\ -3x+y=4\end{array}\right\}$

(c) $\left.\begin{array}{l}-x+y=5 \\ -4x-y=5\end{array}\right\}$

(d) $\left.\begin{array}{l}-3x+\ y=3 \\ 3x+4y=7\end{array}\right\}$

(e) $\left.\begin{array}{l}x-3y=5 \\ -x-4y=9\end{array}\right\}$

(f) $\left.\begin{array}{l}x+3y=15 \\ -x-4y=-9\end{array}\right\}$

2 Solve the following simultaneous equations.

(a) $\left.\begin{array}{l}2x+3y=7 \\ x+3y=5\end{array}\right\}$

(b) $\left.\begin{array}{l}5x-y=4 \\ -3x-y=4\end{array}\right\}$

(c) $\left.\begin{array}{l}-x-2y=3 \\ -3x-2y=5\end{array}\right\}$

(d) $\left.\begin{array}{l}3x+5y=\ 3 \\ 3x+4y=-3\end{array}\right\}$

(e) $\left.\begin{array}{l}-x-3y=5 \\ -x-4y=9\end{array}\right\}$

(f) $\left.\begin{array}{l}-2x+3y=15 \\ -2x-4y=-6\end{array}\right\}$

12.3 Solving harder simultaneous equations

So far, except for the example at the start of the chapter, you have always been able to eliminate one of the unknown letters by adding or subtracting the equations.

If you can't add or subtract to eliminate one of the letters, then you have to multiply one or both of the equations first to get the numbers multiplying one of the unknowns to be the same. Then you can eliminate that unknown.

Example 12.3.1

Solve the equations $\left.\begin{array}{l}2x+3y=5\\x-2y=6\end{array}\right\}$.

$$\left.\begin{array}{l}2x+3y=5\\x-2y=6\end{array}\right\} \quad \begin{array}{l}①\\②\end{array}$$

$$2x-4y=12 \qquad ③$$

$$7y=-7$$

$$y=-1.$$

$$x-2\times(-1)=6$$

$$x=4.$$

The solution is $x=4, y=-1$.

Multiply Equation ② by 2 to make the numbers multiplying x the same.

Subtract Equation ③ from Equation ①.

Solve the resulting equation for y.

Substitute in the simpler equation, Equation ②, to find x.

Check the solution in the other equation, in this case Equation ①.
$2\times4+3\times(-1)=8-3=5 \checkmark$

Sometimes you need to multiply both of the original equations in order to eliminate one of the unknowns.

Example 12.3.2

Solve the equations $\left.\begin{array}{l}2x+3y=-1\\7x-5y=12\end{array}\right\}$.

$$\left.\begin{array}{l}2x+3y=-1\\7x-5y=12\end{array}\right\} \quad \begin{array}{l}①\\②\end{array}$$

$$14x+21y=-7 \qquad ③$$

$$14x-10y=24 \qquad ④$$

$$31y=-31$$

$$y=-1.$$

$$2x+3\times(-1)=-1$$

$$2x-3=-1$$

$$2x=2$$

$$x=1.$$

The solution is $x=1, y=-1$.

Multiply Equation ① by 7 and Equation ② by 2 to make the numbers multiplying x the same.

The numbers multiplying x are now the same, and subtracting Equation ④ from Equation ③ eliminates x.

The solution now proceeds as before.

Check the solution in the other equation.
$7\times1-5\times(-1)=7+5=12 \checkmark$

You could also have solved these simultaneous equations by multiplying Equation ① by 5 and Equation ② by 3 and adding to get $31x=31$.

Example 12.3.3

Solve the simultaneous equations $\left.\begin{array}{l} 0.3x + 3y = 2.7 \\ 0.2x - 7y = 0 \end{array}\right\}$.

$\left.\begin{array}{l} 0.3x + 3y = 2.7 \\ 0.2x - 7y = 0 \end{array}\right\}$ *Start by multiplying both equations by 10 to get rid of the decimals.*

$\left.\begin{array}{l} 3x + 30y = 27 \\ 2x - 70y = 0 \end{array}\right\}$ ①   *Now multiply Equation ① by 2 and*
                ②   *Equation ② by 3 to make the numbers multiplying x both equal to 6.*

$6x + 60y = 54$ ③

$6x - 210y = 0$ ④   *Subtract Equation ④ from Equation ③, and then proceed as before.*

$270y = 54$

$y = 0.2.$ *y is given as a decimal as the original equations included decimals.*

$2x - 70 \times 0.2 = 0$

$2x - 14 = 0$

$2x = 14$

$x = 7.$ *Check the solution in the other equation.*

The solution is $x = 7, y = 0.2.$ $0.3 \times 7 + 3 \times 0.2 = 2.1 + 0.6 = 2.7$ ✓

Example 12.3.4

Solve the simultaneous equations $\left.\begin{array}{l} 3x = 27 - 2y \\ 7y = x \end{array}\right\}$.

$\left.\begin{array}{l} 3x = 27 - 2y \\ 7y = x \end{array}\right\}$ *Start by rearranging the equations into the more usual form.*

$3x + 2y = 27$ ①

$x - 7y = 0$ ②   *Then multiply Equation ② by 3 to make the numbers multiplying x both equal to 3.*

$3x - 21y = 0$ ③

$23y = 27$ *The solution then proceeds in exactly the same way as in the earlier examples.*

$y = \frac{27}{23}.$

$x = 7 \times \frac{27}{23}$

$= \frac{189}{23}.$

The solution is $x = \frac{189}{23}, y = \frac{27}{23}.$

Exercise 12C

1 Solve the following pairs of simultaneous equations.

(a) $\left.\begin{array}{l} x+3y=\ \ 2 \\ 4x+2y=14 \end{array}\right\}$

(b) $\left.\begin{array}{l} -2x+3y=11 \\ -4x+5y=19 \end{array}\right\}$

(c) $\left.\begin{array}{l} 5x+3y=-1 \\ 4x+9y=19 \end{array}\right\}$

(d) $\left.\begin{array}{l} 2x-3y=4 \\ 4x+\ \ y=1 \end{array}\right\}$

(e) $\left.\begin{array}{l} 20x-30y=\ \ 20 \\ 40x-10y=190 \end{array}\right\}$

(f) $\left.\begin{array}{l} 3x-4y=13 \\ 6x+5y=52 \end{array}\right\}$

(g) $\left.\begin{array}{l} 3x+2y=12 \\ 4x+5y=23 \end{array}\right\}$

(h) $\left.\begin{array}{l} 5x-2y=16 \\ 3x-5y=\ \ 2 \end{array}\right\}$

(i) $\left.\begin{array}{l} 4x-\ 3y=\ \ 13 \\ -3x+4y=-15 \end{array}\right\}$

2 Solve the following pairs of simultaneous equations.

(a) $\left.\begin{array}{l} \frac{1}{2}x+\ 3y=7 \\ 4x+\frac{1}{2}y=9 \end{array}\right\}$

(b) $\left.\begin{array}{l} 0.3x+1.2y=1.8 \\ 0.4x+1.5y=2.3 \end{array}\right\}$

(c) $\left.\begin{array}{l} 16x+51y=13 \\ 5x+16y=4 \end{array}\right\}$

(d) $\left.\begin{array}{l} 2x+2y=1 \\ 6x+\ \ y=2 \end{array}\right\}$

(e) $\left.\begin{array}{l} 6x+y=\ \ \ 0 \\ 2x+y=0.4 \end{array}\right\}$

(f) $\left.\begin{array}{l} 3x+2y=2 \\ 5x-\ \ y=2.25 \end{array}\right\}$

(g) $\left.\begin{array}{l} 2x+3y=-\frac{4}{3} \\ x-2y=\ \ \ \frac{5}{3} \end{array}\right\}$

(h) $\left.\begin{array}{l} x=2y-1 \\ 2x=-1-4y \end{array}\right\}$

(i) $\left.\begin{array}{l} 0.3x+0.4y=-0.03 \\ 0.2x-0.3y=\ \ 0.32 \end{array}\right\}$

12.4 Some important results to remember

To solve a pair of simultaneous equations:

- multiply the equations so that the numbers multiplying one of the unknowns are the same or differ only in sign;

- add or subtract the equations to eliminate one of the unknowns;

- solve the resulting equation for the remaining unknown, and then go back to the simpler equation to find the first unknown;

- check your answers.

Test exercise 12

1 Solve the following pairs of simultaneous equations.

(a) $\left.\begin{array}{l} x-y=\ \ 8 \\ x+y=13 \end{array}\right\}$

(b) $\left.\begin{array}{l} x+2y=17 \\ 2x+3y=16 \end{array}\right\}$

(c) $\left.\begin{array}{l} 5x-8y=\ \ \ 4 \\ 2x+3y=-17 \end{array}\right\}$

(d) $\left.\begin{array}{l} 2x-4y=6 \\ 2x+4y=6 \end{array}\right\}$

(e) $\left.\begin{array}{l} 5x=1-4y \\ 5y=1-6x \end{array}\right\}$

(f) $\left.\begin{array}{l} 0.2x-\frac{1}{2}y=-1 \\ 0.1x+\frac{1}{5}y=\ \ 4 \end{array}\right\}$

13 Trigonometry

The first part of this chapter is probably revision, but the second part, about sine and cosine for obtuse angles may be new. When you have completed it you should

- be able to solve trigonometric problems involving right-angled triangles
- know the shapes of the sine and cosine graphs for angles between 0 and 180°
- know that when x is between 90 and 180, $\sin x° = \sin(180 - x)°$ and $\cos x° = -\cos(180 - x)°$.

13.1 Pythagoras's theorem

Pythagoras's theorem states:

> In a right-angled triangle, the square of the length of the side opposite the right angle is equal to the sum of the squares of the lengths of the other two sides.

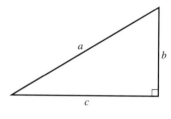

Fig. 13.1

That is, in Fig. 13.1, $a^2 = b^2 + c^2$.

Pythagoras's theorem enables you to calculate the third side of a right-angled triangle if you know the lengths of the other two sides.

13.2 Sine, cosine and tangent

Suppose that you have a right-angled triangle, shown in Fig. 13.2. The side opposite the right angle is called the **hypotenuse**.

In Fig. 13.2, one angle is labelled $\theta°$. (θ is a Greek letter, called 'theta', which is often used to stand for an unknown angle.)

The side opposite $\theta°$ is called the **opposite**; the third side is the **adjacent**.

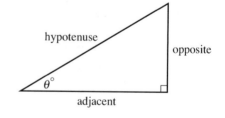

Fig. 13.2

You can't tell which side is the opposite and which the adjacent until you have decided which angle you are interested in.

The trigonometric ratios, $\sin\theta°$, $\cos\theta°$ and $\tan\theta°$, are given by

$$\sin\theta° = \frac{\text{opposite}}{\text{hypotenuse}}, \qquad \cos\theta° = \frac{\text{adjacent}}{\text{hypotenuse}}, \qquad \tan\theta° = \frac{\text{opposite}}{\text{adjacent}}.$$

The values of $\sin\theta°$, $\cos\theta°$ and $\tan\theta°$ depend only on the shape of the triangle, and not on its size.

When tackling questions about right-angled triangles, follow these steps:

- draw a clear diagram, which need not be to scale
- label any known sides or angles, including the right angle
- label any sides or angles you need to find, using x or θ as appropriate
- identify which two of the three sides (opposite, adjacent and hypotenuse) are involved
- decide which ratio, sin, cos or tan, to use
- write down a formula, and substitute into it
- use a calculator to calculate the answer.

Example 13.2.1

In triangle ABC, angle $B = 90°$, angle $C = 26°$ and $AC = 35$ cm. Find the length AB.

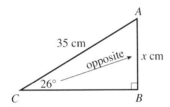

Let $AB = x$ cm.

Using $\sin\theta° = \dfrac{\text{opposite}}{\text{hypotenuse}}$,

$$\sin 26° = \frac{x}{35},$$

$$x = 35\sin 26°$$

$$= 15.34\ldots.$$

The length AB is 15.3 cm, correct to 3 significant figures.

Draw a clear diagram showing all the information you are given, and label the unknown side as x cm.

AC is the hypotenuse. $C = 26°$ is the only angle involved, so AB is the opposite.

The sides involved are the opposite and hypotenuse, so use $\sin\theta° = \dfrac{\text{opposite}}{\text{hypotenuse}}$.

To go from $\sin 26° = \dfrac{x}{35}$ to $x = 35\sin 26°$ multiply both sides by 35. See Section 7.3.

In many cases you can skip the step $\sin\theta° = \dfrac{\text{opposite}}{\text{hypotenuse}}$ and immediately write down $\sin 26° = \dfrac{x}{35}$ or even $x = 35\sin 26°$, but you are advised to put in the step to begin with.

In the next examples, the right angle is not in the bottom right-hand corner of the triangle. You should still be able to identify the hypotenuse, adjacent and opposite, and use the same method as in Example 13.2.1.

Example 13.2.2

In triangle PQR, $PR = 10$ cm, $QR = 12$ cm and angle R is $90°$. Calculate the angle P.

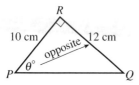

Let angle P be $\theta°$.

Using $\tan\theta° = \dfrac{\text{opposite}}{\text{adjacent}}$,

$\tan\theta° = \dfrac{12}{10} = 1.2$, and

$\theta = 50.19\ldots$.

Angle P is $50.2°$, correct to the nearest 0.1 degrees.

The angle at P is labelled $\theta°$.

As $\theta°$ is the angle you are interested in, QR is the opposite and PR is the adjacent.

As $\tan\theta° = \dfrac{\text{opposite}}{\text{adjacent}}$, use $\tan\theta°$.

The step from $\tan\theta° = 1.2$ to $\theta = 50.19\ldots$ uses either INV TAN, ARC TAN or TAN^{-1} depending on your calculator.

When working in degrees, it is usual to give answers correct to the nearest 0.1 of a degree.

Example 13.2.3

In triangle XYZ, angle $Y = 90°$, angle $X = 50°$ and $XY = 14$ cm. Calculate the lengths YZ and XZ.

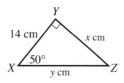

Using $\tan\theta° = \dfrac{\text{opposite}}{\text{adjacent}}$

$\tan 50° = \dfrac{x}{14}$, giving

$x = 14\tan 50° = 16.68\ldots$.

Similarly,

$\cos 50° = \dfrac{14}{y}$

$y\cos 50° = 14$

$y = \dfrac{14}{\cos 50°} = 21.78\ldots$.

$XZ = 21.8$ cm and $YZ = 16.7$ cm correct to 3 significant figures.

Label the unknown sides x cm and y cm.

The angle given is $50°$, XY is the adjacent and x cm is the opposite.

As $\tan\theta° = \dfrac{\text{opposite}}{\text{adjacent}}$, use $\tan\theta°$.

Multiply both sides by 14.

Multiply both sides by y.

Divide both sides by $\cos 50°$.

You could also use Pythagoras's theorem if you prefer.

$14^2 + 16.68\ldots^2 = y^2$, *giving*

$y^2 = 474.37\ldots$

$y = 21.78\ldots.$

Exercise 13A

1 In each part of this question the angle $\theta°$ is labelled. In each part, identify the hypotenuse, the opposite and the adjacent.

(a)

$\theta°$
q cm
p cm
r cm

(b)

l cm
n cm
m cm
$\theta°$

(c)

z cm
x cm
$\theta°$
y cm

(d)

b cm
$\theta°$
a cm
c cm

(e)

r cm
s cm
$\theta°$
t cm

(f)

$\theta°$
e cm
f cm
d cm

2 In each part of this question, find the side or angle marked with a letter. The diagrams are not drawn to scale.

(a)

$\theta°$
10 cm
5 cm

(b)

9 cm
4 cm
$\theta°$

(c)

5 cm
$\theta°$
8 cm

(d)

60°
7 cm
c cm

(e)

s cm
20°
12 cm

(f)

30°
7 cm
d cm

3 All parts of this question refer to a triangle LMN.
   (a) If angle $M = 90°$, $N = 20°$ and $LN = 15$ cm, find the length MN.
   (b) If angle $M = 90°$, $LN = 35$ cm, $MN = 20$ cm, find the angle L.
   (c) If angle $M = 90°$, $L = 40°$, $MN = 20$ cm, find the length LN.
   (d) If angle $L = 90°$, $LN = 6$ cm, $LM = 9$ cm, find the angle M.
   (e) If angle $L = 90°$, $M = 30°$, $LM = 9$ cm, find the length MN.
   (f) If angle $L = 90°$, $M = 30°$, $LM = 9$ cm, find the length LN.

4 In each part of this question, find the side marked with a letter.

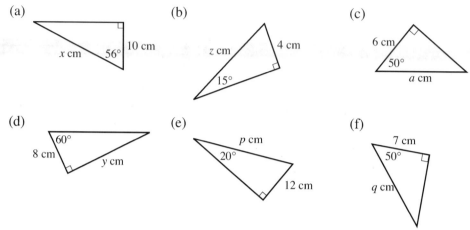

(a)   (b)   (c)

(d)   (e)   (f)

13.3 Trigonometric ratios of obtuse angles

You will find in A level textbooks that $\sin\theta°$ and $\cos\theta°$ can be defined for **obtuse angles**, that is angles greater than 90°. However, the $\dfrac{\text{opposite}}{\text{hypotenuse}}$ and $\dfrac{\text{adjacent}}{\text{hypotenuse}}$ definitions of $\sin\theta°$ and $\cos\theta°$, which involve a right-angled triangle, only work for **acute angles**, that is angles less than 90°.

Defining $\sin\theta°$ and $\cos\theta°$ for obtuse angles is beyond the scope of this book, but you can get important information from your calculator.

You should find Exercise 13B quite straightforward.

Exercise 13B

1 Use your calculator to find the following. What can you deduce from your answers?

    (a) $\sin 20°$, $\sin 160°$ (b) $\sin 30°$, $\sin 150°$ (c) $\sin 35°$, $\sin 145°$

    (d) $\sin 31°$, $\sin 149°$ (e) $\sin 43°$, $\sin 137°$ (f) $\sin 2°$, $\sin 178°$

2 Find the following pairs of values of $\cos\theta°$. What can you deduce from your answers?

    (a) $\cos 20°$, $\cos 160°$ (b) $\cos 30°$, $\cos 150°$ (c) $\cos 35°$, $\cos 145°$

    (d) $\cos 31°$, $\cos 149°$ (e) $\cos 43°$, $\cos 137°$ (f) $\cos 2°$, $\cos 178°$

13.4 The graph of $y = \sin\theta°$

Question 1 in Exercise 13B leads to the following result.

$$\sin\theta° = \sin(180-\theta)° \text{ for all values of } \theta \text{ in the interval } 0 < \theta < 180.$$

If you draw the graph of $y = \sin\theta°$ using values from your calculator, you get the graph shown in Fig. 13.3.

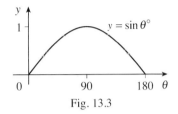
Fig. 13.3

If you use this graph to solve the equation $\sin\theta° = 0.2$ in the interval $0 < \theta < 180$, you find that there are two values of θ, shown in Fig. 13.4.

One of these is the acute angle 11.5 that you get when you use your calculator to find the angle which has a sine equal to 0.2.

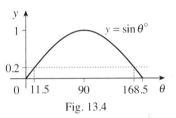
Fig. 13.4

You find the other angle by calculating $180 - 11.5 = 168.5$. You can also check that it is correct by finding its sine from your calculator.

Example 13.4.1
Solve the equation $\sin\theta° = 0.6$ for values of θ lying between 0 and 180.

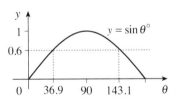

From the calculator, if $\sin\theta° = 0.6$, then $\theta = 36.9$, correct to 1 decimal place.

The other root is $180 - 36.9 = 143.1$.

So $\theta = 36.9$ or 143.1, correct to 1 decimal place.

This uses the property that if θ is a root, so is $180 - \theta$.

13.5 The graph of $y = \cos\theta°$

Question 2 in Exercise 13B leads to the following result.

$$\cos\theta° = -\cos(180-\theta)° \text{ for all values of } \theta \text{ in the interval } 0 < \theta < 180.$$

If you draw the graph of $y = \cos\theta°$, you get the graph shown in Fig. 13.5.

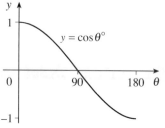

Fig. 13.5

If you use your graph to solve the equation $\cos\theta° = 0.7$ in the interval $0 < \theta < 180$, you find that there is only one value of θ. This is shown in Fig. 13.6

And if $\cos\theta° = -0.7$, there is still just one value of θ, which lies between 90 and 180. (See Example 13.5.1.)

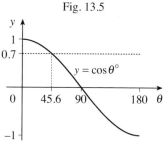

Fig. 13.6

Example 13.5.1

Solve the equation $\cos\theta° = -0.7$ for values of θ lying between 0 and 180.

From the calculator, if $\cos\theta° = -0.7$, then $\theta = 134.4$, correct to 1 decimal place.

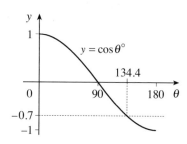

Exercise 13C

1 In each part, find the solution of the equation which lies between 90 and 180.

   (a) $\sin\theta° = 0.5$ (b) $\sin\theta° = 0.3$ (c) $\sin\theta° = \frac{1}{2}\sqrt{3}$

2 Find another angle in the interval between 0 and 180 which has the same sine as the given angle.

   (a) 30   (b) 18.1   (c) 135

3 Solve the following equations, giving all roots between 0 and 180.

   (a) $\cos\theta° = -0.3$ (b) $\sin\theta° = 0.123$ (c) $\cos\theta° = 0.3$
   (d) $\sin\theta° = 0.15$ (e) $\cos\theta° = 0$ (f) $\sin\theta° = 1$

13.6 Some important results to remember

To calculate sides and angles in right-angled triangles use:

$$\sin\theta° = \frac{\text{opposite}}{\text{hypotenuse}}, \qquad \cos\theta° = \frac{\text{adjacent}}{\text{hypotenuse}}, \qquad \tan\theta° = \frac{\text{opposite}}{\text{adjacent}}.$$

For obtuse angles:

$$\sin\theta° = \sin(180-\theta)°, \qquad \cos\theta° = -\cos(180-\theta)°.$$

There are two roots to the equation $\sin\theta° = k$, where $0 < k < 1$ and θ lies in the interval between 0 and 180.

Test exercise 13

1 In each of the following triangles, find the required sides and angles, giving your answers correct to 3 significant figures or to 1 decimal place, as appropriate.

(a) $B = 90°$, $b = 7.3\,\text{cm}$, $C = 10°$: find a and c.

(b) $X = 90°$, $y = 4.3\,\text{cm}$, $z = 4.5\,\text{cm}$: find x and Y.

2 Find the solution(s) in the interval between 0 and 180 to each of the following equations, giving your answers correct to 1 decimal place.

(a) $\cos\theta° = 0.4$ (b) $\cos\theta° = -0.4$ (c) $\sin\theta° = 0.4$

(d) $\sin\theta° = 0$ (e) $\sin\theta° = 0.8$ (f) $\sin\theta° = \frac{1}{2}\sqrt{2}$

14 The sine rule for a triangle

This chapter introduces the sine rule which enables you to use trigonometry to calculate sides and angles in triangles which are not right-angled. When you have completed it you should

- know the formula $\frac{1}{2}ab\sin C$ for the area of a triangle

- know and be able to use the sine rule for a triangle, $\dfrac{a}{\sin A} = \dfrac{b}{\sin B} = \dfrac{c}{\sin C}$

  $\left(\text{or } \dfrac{\sin A}{a} = \dfrac{\sin B}{b} = \dfrac{\sin C}{c}\right).$

14.1 Labelling triangles

If you have a triangle ABC, there is a useful convention that the sides are labelled a, b and c with the side labelled a opposite to the angle A. The sides b and c are opposite the angles B and C.

So small letters are used for sides and capital letters for angles.

This is illustrated in Fig. 14.1.

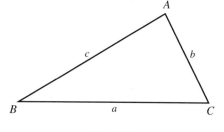

Fig. 14.1

The idea is extended to triangles labelled with other letters, so you would expect a triangle XYZ to have sides labelled x, y and z, with side x opposite the angle X, and so on.

When you use the sides and angles labelled in this way, they do not usually have units attached to them. However, you can assume that the sides are all measured in the same units, and that the angles are measured in degrees.

14.2 Area of a triangle

The purpose of this section is to find a formula for the area of a triangle in terms of the sides and angles of the triangle. You don't need to learn how to derive this result, but you do need to know and be able to use the formula at the top of page 96.

There are two cases which must be considered: acute-angled triangles and obtuse-angled triangles.

You already know the formula

$$\text{area of a triangle} = \tfrac{1}{2} \times \text{base} \times \text{height}.$$

Fig. 14.2 shows this for acute-angled and obtuse-angled triangles.

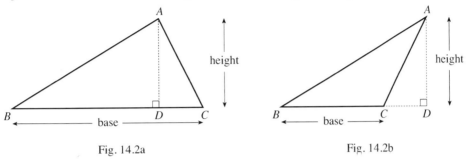

Fig. 14.2a   Fig. 14.2b

In both cases the area of the triangle is denoted by the triangle-shaped symbol Δ, called 'delta', which is the Greek capital D.

Acute-angled triangle   **Obtuse-angled triangle**

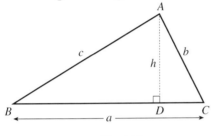 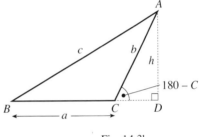

Fig. 14.3a   Fig. 14.3b

Let the height of the triangle be h.

Then, using $\frac{1}{2} \times \text{base} \times \text{height}$,

$$\Delta = \tfrac{1}{2}ah.$$

But, in the triangle ACD,

$$\sin C = \frac{h}{b}, \text{ so } h = b\sin C.$$

Substituting this into the formula for Δ,

$$\Delta = \tfrac{1}{2}ab\sin C.$$

Let the height of the triangle be h.

Then, using $\frac{1}{2} \times \text{base} \times \text{height}$,

$$\Delta = \tfrac{1}{2}ah.$$

But, in the triangle ACD,

$$h = b\sin(180 - C).$$

Substituting this into the formula for Δ,

$$\Delta = \tfrac{1}{2}ab\sin(180 - C).$$

From Section 13.4 and Exercise 13B, for any angle it is true that

$$\sin(180 - C) = \sin C.$$

So $\Delta = \tfrac{1}{2}ab\sin C$.

Regardless of whether the triangle is acute-angled or obtuse-angled,

$$\Delta = \tfrac{1}{2}ab\sin C.$$

You can also prove in a similar way, by starting from a different side as the base of the triangle, that $\Delta = \frac{1}{2}bc\sin A = \frac{1}{2}ac\sin B$.

The area of a triangle is given by

$$\Delta = \tfrac{1}{2}bc\sin A = \tfrac{1}{2}ac\sin B = \tfrac{1}{2}ab\sin C.$$

Example 14.2.1

In triangle ABC, angle $C = 40°$, $AC = 10\,\text{cm}$ and $BC = 12\,\text{cm}$. Calculate the area of the triangle, giving your answer correct to 3 significant figures.

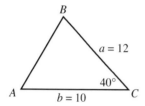

Draw a figure.

From the information given, $a = 12$ and $b = 10$, and you know that $C = 40$.

You need to pick the correct formula, in this case involving the angle C.

Using the formula $\Delta = \tfrac{1}{2}ab\sin C$,

$$\Delta = \tfrac{1}{2} \times 12 \times 10 \times \sin 40°$$

$$= 38.567\ldots.$$

Use your calculator to evaluate the answer.

The required area is $38.6\,\text{cm}^2$, correct to 3 significant figures.

Example 14.2.2

In triangle XYZ, angle $Y = 130°$, $XY = 15\,\text{cm}$ and $ZY = 16\,\text{cm}$. Calculate its area.

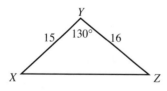

Draw a figure.

From the information given, $x = 16$, $z = 15$ and you know the angle Y.

You need the correct formula, adapted for triangle XYZ, involving the angle Y.

Using the formula $\Delta = \tfrac{1}{2}xz\sin Y$,

$$\Delta = \tfrac{1}{2} \times 16 \times 15 \times \sin 130°$$

$$= 91.925\ldots.$$

Use your calculator to evaluate the answer.

The required area is $91.9\,\text{cm}^2$, correct to 3 significant figures.

Example 14.2.3

In triangle ABC, $b = 10$ and $c = 20$, the units being centimetres. The area of the triangle is $40 \, \text{cm}^2$. Calculate the possible values of the angle A.

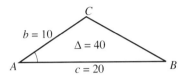

Draw a triangle (not to scale), and label the sides.

From the information given, $b = 10$, $c - 20$ and $\Delta - 40$.

Using the formula $\Delta = \frac{1}{2} bc \sin A$,

Choose the correct formula for area.

$$40 = \tfrac{1}{2} \times 10 \times 20 \times \sin A^\circ$$

$$40 = 100 \sin A^\circ$$

$$\sin A^\circ = 0.4.$$

From your calculator,

Find the first value for the angle A from your calculator.

$$A = 23.578\ldots$$

so angle $A = 23.6°$, correct to 1 decimal place,

However, from Section 13.4, there are two roots, the other being

$$A = 180 - 23.578\ldots = 156.42\ldots$$

$$= 156.4,$$

The second answer is $180 - A$.

correct to 1 decimal place.

The two angles are $23.6°$ and $156.4°$.

The two answers to Example 14.2.3, angle $A = 23.6°$ and $156.4°$, correspond to the two triangles which have sides 10 cm, 20 cm and area $40 \, \text{cm}^2$. These are shown in Fig. 14.4, which is drawn to scale. You can see that they have the same base, 20 cm, and the same height.

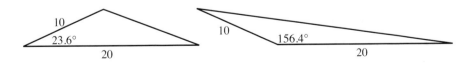

Fig. 14.4

────────────────────────────────

Exercise 14A

────────────────────────────────

1 Find the areas of the following triangles. In each case, two sides and the angle between them are given.

    (a) 13 cm, 24 cm, 30°   (b) 4 cm, 12 cm, 130°   (c) 4 cm, 3 cm, 90°

    (d) 6 cm, 7 cm, 150°   (e) 2 cm, 2 cm, 2°   (f) 8 cm, 4 cm, 60°

2 Find the area of the triangle ABC given the following information, where the units are centimetres.

    (a) $b = 3.4$, $c = 5.6$, angle $A = 72°$ (b) $a = 5$, $b = 7$, angle $C = 15°$

3 In each part of this question, the area of the triangle is 40 cm^2. The lengths of two sides are given. Calculate the two possible angles between those sides. In one of the parts, the information given is inconsistent. Identify this part.

    (a) 10 cm, 15 cm   (b) 20 cm, 15 cm   (c) 9 cm, 9 cm

    (d) 8 cm, 8 cm   (e) 4 cm, 40 cm   (f) 9 cm, 19 cm

────────────────────────────────

14.3 The sine rule for a triangle

The formula

$$\Delta = \tfrac{1}{2}bc \sin A = \tfrac{1}{2}ac \sin B = \tfrac{1}{2}ab \sin C$$

for the area of triangle ABC (Fig. 14.5) leads to a useful result called the sine rule.

Starting with the equation

$$\tfrac{1}{2}bc \sin A = \tfrac{1}{2}ac \sin B = \tfrac{1}{2}ab \sin C$$

multiply by 2 and divide by abc to get

$$\frac{\sin A}{a} = \frac{\sin B}{b} = \frac{\sin C}{c}.$$

You can write this in the alternative form

$$\frac{a}{\sin A} = \frac{b}{\sin B} = \frac{c}{\sin C}.$$

This is called **the sine rule**.

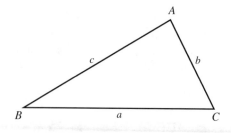

Fig. 14.5

You may need to modify the lettering for a particular triangle, but in practice this is easy to do.

Example 14.3.1
Find the length marked b in the figure opposite.

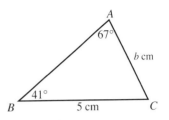

In triangle ABC, you know that $a = 5$, and you need to find b.

Using $\dfrac{a}{\sin A} = \dfrac{b}{\sin B}$,

Choose the relevant part of the sine rule.

$$\frac{5}{\sin 67°} = \frac{b}{\sin 41°},$$

Substitute the given values.

Rearrange to find b.

$$b = \frac{5\sin 41°}{\sin 67°} = 3.563\ldots.$$

Use your calculator, keeping all the significant figures in intermediate calculations.

The length is 3.56 cm, correct to 3 significant figures.

Example 14.3.2
In triangle PQR, $PQ = 6\,\text{cm}$, and angles P and Q are 50° and 60° respectively. Find the length QR.

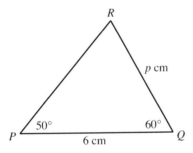

Draw a figure.

In triangle PQR, you know that $r = 6$, and you need to find p.

$$R = 180 - 50 - 60 = 70.$$

Using $\dfrac{p}{\sin P} = \dfrac{r}{\sin R}$,

$$\frac{p}{\sin 50°} = \frac{6}{\sin 70°}$$

$$p = \frac{6\sin 50°}{\sin 70°} = 4.891\ldots.$$

The length QR is 4.89 cm, correct to 3 significant figures.

The problem here is that you do not know the angle R opposite PQ. However, you know that the angles of a triangle add up to 180°, so you can work out R from the other two angles.

Then the solution proceeds as for Example 14.3.1.

Example 14.3.3

Find the angle Z in the figure opposite.

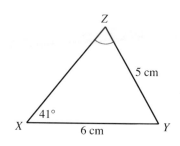

Using $\dfrac{\sin X}{x} = \dfrac{\sin Z}{z}$, $\dfrac{\sin 41°}{5} = \dfrac{\sin Z°}{6}$,

giving

$$\sin Z° = \frac{6\sin 41°}{5}$$

$$Z = 51.9 \text{ or } 128.1,$$

correct to 1 decimal place.

x = 5 and z = 6 in this triangle.

Both solutions are possible: one triangle has angles $41°$, $51.9°$ and $87.1°$; the other has angles $41°$, $128.1°$ and $10.9°$.

Angle $Z = 51.9°$ or $128.1°$.

You must check both roots; Example 14.3.4 shows why.

The two triangles are shown in Fig. 14.6.

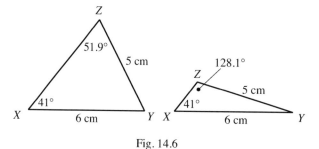

Fig. 14.6

Example 14.3.4

Find the angle B in the figure opposite.

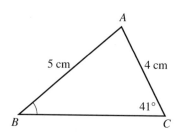

Using $\dfrac{\sin B}{b} = \dfrac{\sin C}{c}$, $\dfrac{\sin B°}{4} = \dfrac{\sin 41°}{5}$,

so $\quad \sin B° = \dfrac{4\sin 41°}{5} = 0.5248\ldots,$

$$B = 31.7 \text{ or } 148.3,$$

correct to 1 decimal place.

b = 4 and c = 5 in this triangle.

If $B = 31.7$, one triangle has angles $41°$, $31.7°$ and $180° - 41° - 31.7° = 97.3°$.
If $B = 148.3$, the other triangle has angles $41°$, $148.3°$, and $180° - 41° - 148.3° = -9.3°$ which is impossible.

The only solution is angle $B = 31.7°$.

This example shows the importance of checking both roots of the equation.

Exercise 14B

1 In each part, find the length of the marked side.

(a)

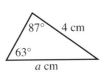

(b)

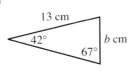

(c)

(d)

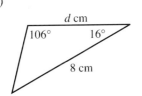

(e)

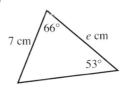

(f)

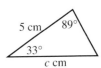

2 In each part, find the possible value or values of the marked angle.

(a)

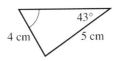

(b)

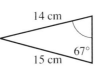

(c)

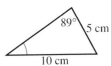

(d)

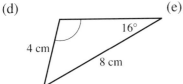

(e)

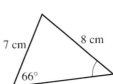

(f)

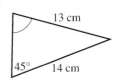

14.4 Some important results to remember

The area Δ of a triangle is given by

$$\Delta = \tfrac{1}{2} bc \sin A = \tfrac{1}{2} ac \sin B = \tfrac{1}{2} ab \sin C .$$

The sine rule for a triangle is

$$\frac{a}{\sin A} = \frac{b}{\sin B} = \frac{c}{\sin C} .$$

When you use the sine rule to find an angle, there may be two solutions.

Test exercise 14

1 Find the areas of the following triangles, giving your answers correct to 3 significant figures.

   (a) $x = 43\,\text{cm},\ y = 65\,\text{cm},\ Z = 12°$ (b) $a = 11.3\,\text{cm},\ b = 13.5\,\text{cm},\ C = 130°$

2 In each of the following triangles find the lengths of the sides, giving your answers to 3 significant figures.

   (a) $p = 9.2\,\text{cm},\ R = 130°,\ P = 32°$: find q and r.
   (b) $a = 15.3\,\text{cm},\ A = 14°,\ C = 130°$: find b and c.

3 In each of the following triangles find the required angles, giving your answers correct to 1 decimal place.

   (a) $x = 8.5\,\text{cm},\ y = 7.5\,\text{cm},\ X = 82°$: find Y, Z.
   (b) $a = 7.3\,\text{cm},\ c = 5.3\,\text{cm},\ C = 10°$: find A, B.

15 The cosine rule for a triangle

If you are given two sides of a triangle and the angle between them, you cannot use the sine rule to calculate the length of the third side. Similarly, if you know the lengths of the three sides you cannot use the sine rule to calculate the angles. For this you need the subject of this chapter, the cosine rule for a triangle. When you have completed the chapter you should

- know and be able to use the cosine rule for a triangle, $c^2 = a^2 + b^2 - 2ab\cos C$, and the related rules $a^2 = b^2 + c^2 - 2bc\cos A$ and $b^2 = c^2 + a^2 - 2ca\cos B$.

15.1 Derivation of the cosine rule

At a first reading you may omit this derivation, and start at Section 15.2.

Suppose that you know the lengths of the sides a and b of a triangle, and the angle C between them, and you need to find the length of the side c.

This is illustrated in Fig. 15.1. Fig. 15.1a applies when the angle at C is acute, and Fig. 15.1b applies when it is obtuse. In both cases, the side c to be found has been shown dashed.

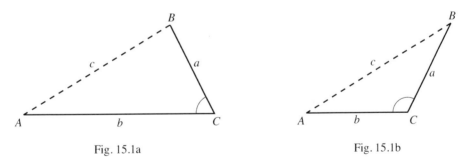

Fig. 15.1a   Fig. 15.1b

It is worth noting that if you are given the lengths of a and b and the angle between them, you could draw the triangle using a ruler and protractor, so it ought to be possible to calculate c in terms of a, b and C.

The sine rule is no help.

In the equation $\dfrac{\sin A}{a} = \dfrac{\sin B}{b} = \dfrac{\mathbf{\sin C}}{c}$ you know just one quantity, shown in bold type, in each part of the rule. If you now try to make c the subject of the rule, you don't seem to get anywhere.

What you have to do is to go back to basics, and create right-angled triangles by dropping perpendiculars from B to AC, meeting it at D. In the acute-angled case, shown in Fig. 15.2a, D is between A and C, while in the obtuse-angled case, it is not between A and C.

These cases need to be dealt with separately, but they are very similar and will end with the same formula.

Let the length BD be h, and the length CD be x.

Acute-angled triangle

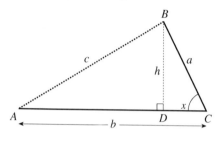

Fig. 15.2a

Obtuse-angled triangle

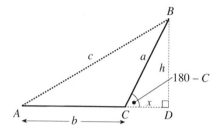

Fig. 15.2b

Using Pythagoras's theorem in triangle ABD,

$$c^2 = (b-x)^2 + h^2$$
$$= b^2 - 2bx + x^2 + h^2.$$

Using Pythagoras's theorem in triangle BDC,

$$a^2 = h^2 + x^2.$$

Substitute from this equation for $h^2 + x^2$ into the equation for c^2:

$$c^2 = b^2 - 2bx + a^2,$$

which you can rearrange as

$$c^2 = a^2 + b^2 - 2bx.$$

In triangle BDC,

$$x = a\cos C.$$

So, substituting this for x,

$$c^2 = a^2 + b^2 - 2ba\cos C,$$

which is the same as

$$c^2 = a^2 + b^2 - 2ab\cos C.$$

Using Pythagoras's theorem in triangle ABD,

$$c^2 = (b+x)^2 + h^2$$
$$= b^2 + 2bx + x^2 + h^2.$$

Using Pythagoras's theorem in triangle BDC,

$$a^2 = h^2 + x^2.$$

Substitute from this equation for $h^2 + x^2$ into the equation for c^2:

$$c^2 = b^2 + 2bx + a^2,$$

which you can rearrange as

$$c^2 = a^2 + b^2 + 2bx.$$

In triangle BDC,

$$x = a\cos(180 - C),$$

which is the same as $x = -a\cos C$.

So, substituting this for x,

$$a^2 = b^2 + c^2 + 2b \times (-a\cos C),$$

which is the same as

$$c^2 = a^2 + b^2 - 2ab\cos C.$$

15.2 Using the cosine rule for a triangle

The formula $c^2 = a^2 + b^2 - 2ab\cos C$ is called **the cosine rule for a triangle**, or sometimes, more briefly, **the cosine rule**.

The rule $c^2 = a^2 + b^2 - 2ab\cos C$ has a resemblance to Pythagoras's theorem (Section 13.1), and is sometimes called the extension of Pythagoras's theorem. Think of the term $2ab\cos C$ as an adjustment which you need if the triangle ABC is not right-angled.

But what happens if you had been given b, c and the angle A and tried to find the length of the side a?

The answer is that b takes the place of a, c takes the place of b, a takes the place of c and A takes the place of C in the formula $c^2 = a^2 + b^2 - 2ab\cos C$, to get

$$a^2 = b^2 + c^2 - 2bc\cos A.$$

Similarly,

$$b^2 = c^2 + a^2 - 2ca\cos B.$$

All of these are variations of the cosine rule.

As with the sine rule, you may need to modify the letters for a particular triangle. For example, the cosine rule for triangle PQR can be written as

$$p^2 = q^2 + r^2 - 2qr\cos P, \quad q^2 = r^2 + p^2 - 2rp\cos Q, \quad r^2 = p^2 + q^2 - 2pq\cos R.$$

The letters a, b, c in the original formulae are replaced by p, q, r respectively.

Example 15.2.1
A triangle ABC has $AB = 3\,\text{cm}$, $BC = 5\,\text{cm}$ and $B = 120°$. Find AC.

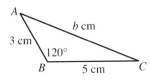

Draw a figure, and identify the variation of the cosine rule that you need. It is usually the one which starts with the side that you are trying to find, in this case b.

Using the cosine rule,
$$b^2 = c^2 + a^2 - 2ca\cos B,$$
$$b^2 = 3^2 + 5^2 - 2\times 3\times 5\cos 120°$$
$$= 9 + 25 - 30\times(-0.5)$$
$$= 9 + 25 + 15$$
$$= 49.$$
$$b = \sqrt{49} = 7.$$

So $AC = 7\,\text{cm}$.

From the diagram $a = 5$ and $c = 3$.

Substitute these values into the rule. Remember BODMAS: do the multiplications before adding.

Note the sign of $\cos 120°$.

The cosine rule can also be used to find angles, given all three sides, as in the next example.

Example 15.2.2

A triangle PQR has $PQ = 4$ cm, $QR = 6$ cm and $PR = 8$ cm. Find angles Q and P.

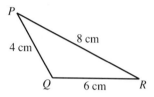

Draw the usual diagram.

From the cosine rule,

$$q^2 = r^2 + p^2 - 2rp\cos Q,$$
$$8^2 = 6^2 + 4^2 - 2 \times 6 \times 4 \cos Q°,$$

so　　$64 = 16 + 36 - 48 \cos Q°,$

giving

$$48\cos Q° = 16 + 36 - 64 = -12,$$

that is $\cos Q° = -\dfrac{1}{4}$.

So　$Q = 104.47... = 104.5$, correct to 1 decimal place.

Angle $Q = 104.5°$.

Using the sine rule,

$$\frac{\sin P}{p} = \frac{\sin Q}{q}$$

giving

$$\sin P° = \frac{6 \times \sin 104.47...°}{8}$$
$$= 0.726....$$

$$P = 46.567... \text{ or } 133.43.$$

As the triangle already has one obtuse angle, you need the acute angle. So angle $P = 46.6°$, correct to 1 decimal place.

When you have to find two angles, always start with the largest angle, which is the one opposite the largest side. The other angles must then all be smaller, a useful check.

To find the angle Q, use the cosine rule which includes $\cos Q$.

From the diagram, $q = 8$, $r = 4$ and $p = 6$.

Having found Q, you could either go back to the original sides and start again to find P, or you could use the sine rule to find it.

In this example, the sine rule is used. It is usually easier. However, if you use the cosine rule, you do not get two possible angles to consider.

Use the most accurate value of Q that you can. If you use the value of Q correct to 1 decimal place, your answer may not be accurate.

Exercise 15A

1 In each of the following triangles, the lengths of two sides and the size of the angle between them are given. In each case find the length of the third side.

(a) 13 cm, 24 cm, 30°   (b) 4 cm, 12 cm, 130°   (c) 4 cm, 3 cm, 90°

(d) 6 cm, 7 cm, 150°   (e) 2 cm, 2 cm, 2°   (f) 8 cm, 4 cm, 60°

2 In each part of this question, the lengths in centimetres of the three sides of the triangle are given. Find the size of the given angle, correct to 1 decimal place. In the very last part, the triangle given is 'impossible'. Try using the cosine rule and see what happens.

(a) $a = 10$, $b = 20$, $c = 15$; B (b) $x = 5$, $y = 6$, $z = 7$; Z

(c) $p = 3$, $q = 4$, $r = 6$; R (d) $l = 3.2$, $m = 1.7$, $n = 4.2$; M

(e) $u = 4.6$, $v = 1.7$, $w = 3.5$; U (f) $d = 2.1$, $e = 3.5$, $f = 7.7$; F

3 In each part of this question, the lengths in centimetres of the three sides of the triangle are given. Find the sizes of the two given angles, correct to 1 decimal place.

(a) $a = 5.1$, $b = 6.3$, $c = 7.4$; B,C (b) $x = 10.4$, $y = 11.1$, $z = 13.3$; Z,X

(c) $p = 3$, $q = 4$, $r = 5$; R,P (d) $l = 4.2$, $m = 2.3$, $n = 2.9$; M,N

(e) $u = 7.3$, $v = 9.2$, $w = 8.6$; U,V (f) $d = 2.1$, $e = 3.5$, $f = 3.2$; D,F

15.3 Some important results to remember

For a triangle ABC, with sides a, b and c, the cosine rule states

$$a^2 = b^2 + c^2 - 2bc \cos A,$$

$$b^2 = c^2 + a^2 - 2ca \cos B$$

and $c^2 = a^2 + b^2 - 2ab \cos C.$

Test exercise 15

1 Find the length of the third side of the triangle in the following two cases.

(a) $x = 3.8$ cm, $y = 5.2$ cm, $Z = 67.3°$

(b) $l = 14.2$ cm, $m = 13.3$ cm, $N = 134.2°$

2 Find all the angles of the triangle whose sides are

(a) 4.2 cm, 5.3 cm, 6.4 cm,   (b) 5.3 cm, 5.2 cm, 9.9 cm.

16 Circle theorems

The angle at the centre of a circle is twice the angle at the circumference.

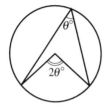 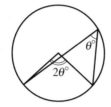 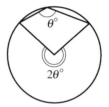

In each case, the angle at the centre marked with two arcs is double the angle at the circumference marked with one arc.

The proof comes from drawing the radius joining the centre to the point on the circumference, and marking all the equal angles produced by the isosceles triangles.

The angle in a semicircle is a right angle.

This follows from the previous result because the angle at the centre is 180°.

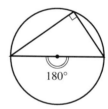

The angles in the same segment are equal.

All angles in the upper part of the circle which are formed by lines from the same chord are equal to each other.

This follows from the first result.

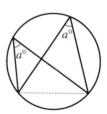

The opposite angles of a cyclic quadrilateral add to 180°.

A **cyclic quadrilateral** is a quadrilateral with all its vertices lying on a circle.

The two angles at the centre add to 360°, so $2a + 2b = 360$.

It follows from the first result that $a + b = 180$.

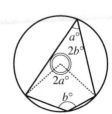

The angle between a tangent and a radius is 90°.

The tangent is the line which just touches
the circle.

The angle between a tangent and a chord is equal to the angle which stands on that chord.

The two angles marked are equal.

This result is usually called the **alternate segment theorem**.

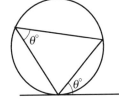

17 Mensuration formulae

Circles

The **length of a circular arc** which subtends an angle of $\theta°$ at the centre of a circle of radius r is $\dfrac{\theta}{360} \times 2\pi r$.

The **area of a circular sector** which subtends an angle of $\theta°$ at the centre of a circle of radius r is $\dfrac{\theta}{360} \times \pi r^2$.

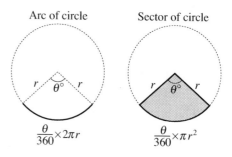

Arc of circle — $\dfrac{\theta}{360} \times 2\pi r$

Sector of circle — $\dfrac{\theta}{360} \times \pi r^2$

Spheres

The **surface area of a sphere** of radius r is $4\pi r^2$.

The **volume of a sphere** of radius r is $\dfrac{4}{3}\pi r^3$.

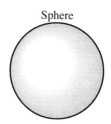

Sphere

Pyramids and cones

The **volume of a pyramid or cone** of vertical height h and base area A, whatever the shape of the base, is $\frac{1}{3}Ah$.

For a right-circular cone, normally simply called a cone, for which $A = \pi r^2$, the formula for volume becomes $V = \frac{1}{3}\pi r^2 h$.

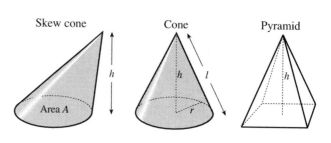

Skew cone — Area A, h

Cone — h, l, r

Pyramid — h

When you multiply out any of these expressions, BODMAS applies. Start by calculating r^2 or r^3, and then multiply by the other quantities.

18 Areas and volumes of similar figures

Suppose that you know that two shapes or solids are mathematically similar, and that one is an exact enlargement of the other, with enlargement scale factor k.

In the diagram, the pumpkin on the right is exactly 3 times the size of the pumpkin on the left, that is, it is 3 times as wide and 3 times as high and 3 times as deep.

In fact, the pumpkin on the right is an enlargement of the pumpkin on the left, with scale factor 3.

So in this case, $k = 3$.

Areas of similar figures

If one shape or solid is an enlargement of another with scale factor k, then the larger shape has an area which is k^2 times the corresponding area of the smaller shape.

Thus the surface area of the larger pumpkin is $3^2 = 9$ times the surface area of the smaller pumpkin.

So if the surface area of the smaller pumpkin is $100\,\text{cm}^2$, then the surface area of the larger pumpkin is $9 \times 100\,\text{cm}^2 = 900\,\text{cm}^2$.

Volumes of similar figures

If one shape or solid is an enlargement of another with scale factor k, then the larger shape has a volume which is k^3 times the corresponding volume of the smaller shape.

Thus the volume of the larger pumpkin is $3^3 = 27$ times the volume of the smaller pumpkin.

So if the volume of the smaller pumpkin is $1000\,\text{cm}^3$, then the volume of the larger pumpkin is $27 \times 1000\,\text{cm}^3 = 27\,000\,\text{cm}^3$.

Answers

1 Starting algebra

Exercise 1A (page 5)

1. (a) 2 (b) $2b+7$ (c) $3c$
   (d) $5d-12$ (e) $7e+1$ (f) f
   (g) 2 (h) 0 (i) $1-i$
   (j) $7g$ (k) f (l) x
   (m) $2y$ (n) $2z-3$
   (o) $2u-1-u^2$

2. (a) $4a+6b$ (b) $3c-7d$
   (c) $4x-4y$ (d) $6x$
   (e) $u+4w$ (f) $7l-2m-3n$

3. (a) $5xy$ (b) $6xy$
   (c) $2ab+2b^2$ (d) $10p^2$
   (e) $16q^2$ (f) $8ab$

4. (a) $2+g^2$ (b) $4h^2-h$
   (c) $2j^2-9j+9$ (d) h^2-2h
   (e) $2l^2+13l+21$ (f) $m-3$

5. (a) p^3 (b) $2q^3$ (c) $6r^3$
   (d) $2s^3$ (e) $12t^3$ (f) $2p^3$
   (g) $5x^2$ (h) $6y^2-4y^3$ (i) 0

6. (a) $4a-2ab$ (b) $2ab$
   (c) $a+b+2ab$ (d) $a^2-ab^2+2a^2b$
   (e) a^2+a^2b (f) 0

Exercise 1B (page 7)

1. (a) 8 (b) -1 (c) -5
   (d) 15 (e) 33 (f) -24
   (g) -1 (h) -30 (i) -40
   (j) -6 (k) 51 (l) 110

2. (a) 1 (b) -9 (c) -25
   (d) -13 (e) -6 (f) 4
   (g) -10 (h) 13 (i) -7
   (j) 7 (k) -45 (l) -99

Test exercise 1 (page 8)

1. (a) $a+b+c$ (b) $3a+b$
   (c) $x-y$ (d) $2lm+l-m$
   (e) $abc-b^2$ (f) $ab+c$
   (g) $a+bc$ (h) $2p^2$
   (i) $3q^3$ (j) $2p^2q^2$
   (k) $16x^2$ (l) $8x^2y^3$

2. (a) -1 (b) -6 (c) -1
   (d) 5 (e) -3 (f) 20
   (g) 25 (h) -12 (i) 0
   (j) 144 (k) 2304 (l) -864

3. 58 m^2

2 Brackets

Exercise 2A (page 10)

1. (a) 10 (b) 7 (c) 7
   (d) 6 (e) 39 (f) 17

2. (a) -2 (b) 38 (c) -14
   (d) 8 (e) -4 (f) -45

3. (a) 18 (b) 18 (c) 1
   (d) -10 (e) -6 (f) 3

4. (a) -4 (b) 12 (c) 4
   (d) -12 (e) 4 (f) 24

Exercise 2B (page 12)

1. (a) $2x+6$ (b) $4y+8$
   (c) $6-3z$ (d) $5t-15$
   (e) $12-8p$ (f) $10p+15q$
   (g) $ac+a$ (h) $2bd+3b$
   (i) $cp-2c$ (j) $dh-5d$
   (k) m^2-2m (l) $3n-n^2$
   (m) $6l-4lm$ (n) $6m^2-12m$
   (o) $2n^3-4n^2$

2. (a) $-2x-6$ (b) $-4y-8$
   (c) $8-2z$ (d) $15-6t$
   (e) $-2ac+2a$ (f) $-6b+4ab$
   (g) $-2c^2+cd$ (h) $-5d+3d^2$
   (i) $-12l+8l^2$ (j) $-4a^2n+3an^2$
   (k) $-6n+4n^2+8n^3$
   (l) $-6m^2+2mn-4mn^2$

3. (a) $2b$ (b) p^2-p
   (c) $2pq-q^2$ (d) $3xy-6x$
   (e) $2x^2-3x+3x^3$ (f) $7x+2x^2+3x^3$
   (g) $2ab-5b$ (h) $3x-6$
   (i) $2ab+4ac-2abc$

4. (a) $3-x$ (b) $a-b-2$
   (c) $3a-b$ (d) p
   (e) $8-a$ (f) -2
   (g) $2ab-ac+c$ (h) $2x+2$
   (i) $m-3n$

Exercise 2C (page 13)

1 (a) $14 - 2a$ (b) $-6b$
(c) -1 (d) $-9 - 45y$
(e) $12x + 4xy$ (f) $-45x - 60xy$
(g) $-6x + 6y$ (h) $4z - 12x - 4xz$
(i) 0 (j) $-pq - 5q^2$
(k) $-ax + bx + abx + bx^2$
(l) $xy + 5y^2$

2 (a) $5bx - ax$ (b) $12py$
(c) $3x^2y + 2xy^2 - x^2y^2$
(d) $30yz - 24xz$
(e) $-4ab + 6a^2b - 2ab^2 - 4abc$
(f) $-5x - 70xy$ (g) $-3x + 6y - 2xy$
(h) $4y - 4yz$
(i) $-xy^2z + 2x^2y - 2x^2z + x^2yz$
(j) $4x^3 - 8x^2$
(k) $-6x^2 + 2x^2y - 2xy$
(l) $-cm + bcm - bx - 2mx + cmx$

3 (a) $7x^2$ (b) $6y^2$
(c) 0 (d) $12z^3$

Test exercise 2 (page 14)

1 (a) -9 (b) 10 (c) 4
(d) 2 (e) 8 (f) 14

2 (a) $a^2 + 2ab + b^2$ (b) $a^2 - 2ab - b^2$
(c) $z^2 - 9$ (d) $-6z^2$
(e) $8x^2$ (f) 0

3 Simple equations

Exercise 3A (page 18)

1 (a) 2 (b) 13 (c) 1
(d) -5 (e) 2 (f) 5
(g) -1 (h) 0 (i) 2
(j) 5 (k) -2 (l) -3

2 (a) 2 (b) -2 (c) 2
(d) -3 (e) -1 (f) 0
(g) 1 (h) -4 (i) -8

Exercise 3B (page 19)

1 (a) 5 (b) 9 (c) 4
(d) 5 (e) -7 (f) 0
(g) 12 (h) 0

2 (a) -5 (b) 5 (c) -2
(d) 2 (e) -20 (f) -6
(g) 2 (h) 1 (i) 5

3 (a) 8 (b) -3 (c) 0
(d) 3 (e) 2 (f) 0

4 (a) -2 (b) 0 (c) 3
(d) 4 (e) -11 (f) -1

Test exercise 3 (page 20)

1 (a) -1 (b) -7 (c) -2
(d) 1 (e) 0 (f) 9

2 (a) 8 (b) 3 (c) -1
(d) -2 (e) 0 (f) 4

4 Fractions in arithmetic

Exercise 4A (page 22)

1 (a) $\frac{2}{5}$ (b) $\frac{7}{2}$ (c) $\frac{11}{6}$ (d) $\frac{5}{4}$
(e) $\frac{8}{4}$ (f) $\frac{12}{3}$ (g) $\frac{5}{2}$ (h) $\frac{5}{7}$

2 (a) $3x = 1$ (b) $9x = 2$
(c) $3p = 8$ (d) $5y = 1$
(e) $7a = 2$ (f) $x = 5$
(g) $3b = 1$ (h) $2z = 3$

Exercise 4B (page 23)

1 (a) $\frac{3}{4}$ (b) $\frac{5}{4}$ (c) $\frac{4}{7}$ (d) $\frac{28}{3}$
(e) $\frac{4}{35}$ (f) $\frac{7}{8}$ (g) $\frac{32}{15}$ (h) $\frac{1}{5}$
(i) $\frac{5}{7}$ (j) $\frac{10}{3}$ (k) $\frac{7}{3}$ (l) $\frac{7}{10}$

2 (a) $\frac{4}{5}$ (b) $\frac{4}{3}$ (c) $\frac{3}{1} = 3$ (d) $\frac{5}{4}$
(e) $\frac{5}{2}$ (f) $\frac{5}{2}$ (g) $\frac{5}{4}$ (h) $\frac{27}{2}$

Exercise 4C (page 25)

1 (a) $\frac{3}{10}$ (b) $\frac{1}{4}$ (c) $\frac{5}{18}$ (d) $\frac{7}{15}$
(e) $\frac{2}{3}$ (f) $\frac{3}{2}$ (g) $\frac{8}{3}$ (h) 10
(i) 1 (j) 3 (k) $\frac{1}{6}$ (l) 1

2 (a) $\frac{3}{2}$ (b) $\frac{1}{2}$ (c) $\frac{32}{15}$ (d) $\frac{3}{4}$
(e) $\frac{9}{4}$ (f) 2 (g) $\frac{2}{9}$ (h) $\frac{1}{4}$
(i) $\frac{8}{3}$ (j) $\frac{5}{8}$ (k) $\frac{1}{6}$ (l) $\frac{3}{2}$

Exercise 4D (page 27)

1 (a) $\frac{7}{40}$ (b) $\frac{23}{12}$ (c) $\frac{43}{36}$ (d) $\frac{3}{10}$
(e) $\frac{17}{21}$ (f) $\frac{67}{60}$ (g) $\frac{161}{72}$ (h) $\frac{13}{72}$

2 (a) $-\frac{11}{30}$ (b) $\frac{5}{12}$ (c) $\frac{1}{20}$ (d) $\frac{1}{5}$

Test exercise 4 (page 28)

1 (a) $\frac{5}{6}$ (b) $\frac{5}{9}$ (c) $\frac{2}{5}$ (d) $\frac{8}{3}$

(e) $\frac{3}{2}$ (f) $\frac{24}{25}$ (g) $\frac{3}{2}$ (h) $\frac{4}{3}$

2 (a) $\frac{11}{10}$ (b) $\frac{5}{28}$ (c) $\frac{9}{4}$ (d) $\frac{7}{12}$

(e) $\frac{17}{20}$ (f) $\frac{5}{84}$ (g) $\frac{5}{8}$ (h) 0

5 Fractions in algebra

Exercise 5A (page 30)

1 (a) $\frac{3y}{2z}$ (b) $\frac{1}{2}q$ (c) $\frac{2}{3}y$

(d) p^2 (e) $\frac{1}{c^2}$ (f) $\frac{1}{2}n^2$

(g) $\frac{8}{5}x^2$ (h) $\frac{1}{6}a$

2 (a) ab^2 (b) $\frac{xy^2}{z^2}$ (c) $\frac{p^2}{q^2r^2}$

(d) $\frac{1}{y}$ (e) $\frac{q^2}{r^2}$ (f) $\frac{y^2}{x}$

(g) 1 (h) $\frac{my}{x}$

3 (a) $\frac{x^2}{4y^2}$ (b) $\frac{4}{n}$ (c) $\frac{y^2}{9x^2}$

(d) $\frac{2x^2}{3y}$ (e) $\frac{1}{8}xy$ (f) $2q$

(g) $\frac{1}{10}x^2y$ (h) $\frac{3}{2}a^2$

Exercise 5B (page 32)

1 (a) x (b) $\frac{a}{b}$ (c) $\frac{1}{q}$

(d) cd (e) $\frac{p^2}{q^2}$ (f) $\frac{12x}{y}$

(g) $\frac{1}{4}y^2$ (h) $\frac{6}{5}uv$

2 (a) $\frac{3}{d}$ (b) $\frac{2h^3}{k^2}$ (c) $\frac{1}{2}l^2$

(d) $\frac{2}{3}q$ (e) $\frac{8}{9b}$ (f) $\frac{2v}{u}$

(g) $\frac{1}{24}x$ (h) $2p$

Exercise 5C (page 33)

1 (a) $\frac{8}{15}x$ (b) $\frac{3}{10}y$ (c) $\frac{1}{6}z$

(d) $\frac{3p-2q}{6}$ (e) $\frac{2x+y}{2}$ (f) $\frac{5}{4}n$

(g) $\frac{7}{15}x$ (h) 0

2 (a) $\frac{5}{x}$ (b) $\frac{16}{3u}$ (c) $\frac{7}{6p}$

(d) $\frac{39}{8y}$ (e) $\frac{7x}{4y}$ (f) $\frac{4j}{3k}$

(g) $\frac{-a}{10b}$ (h) $\frac{7}{4y}$

3 (a) $\frac{1}{2}(a-b)$ (b) $\frac{s^2-2t^2}{2st}$

(c) $\frac{u^2+v^2}{uv}$ (d) $\frac{yz+xz+xy}{xyz}$

(e) $\frac{3x+2}{x^2}$ (f) $\frac{x^3+y^3}{xy}$

(g) $\frac{3xz+4y^2}{yz}$ (h) $\frac{6+x^2}{2x}$

Test exercise 5 (page 34)

1 (a) $\frac{5}{9}$ (b) $\frac{2}{y^3}$ (c) $\frac{6}{xy}$

(d) $2x$ (e) $\frac{3}{2}$ (f) $\frac{2}{x}$

(g) $\frac{2}{3}a$ (h) $\frac{8y}{x}$

2 (a) $\frac{3}{2}$ (b) $\frac{2a+b}{4}$ (c) $\frac{7}{6x}$

(d) $\frac{7p}{3q}$ (e) $\frac{2+n^2}{2n}$ (f) $\frac{3p^2+q^2}{pq}$

(g) $\frac{4x-5}{x}$ (h) $\frac{15x^2-2}{10x}$

3 (a) $\frac{5}{12}$ (b) $\frac{1}{12}x$ (c) $\frac{6}{n}$

(d) $\frac{1}{8}pq$ (e) $\frac{9}{8}$ (f) $\frac{13}{30}$

(g) $\frac{1}{2x}$ (h) $\frac{11}{6}a$

6 Indices

Exercise 6A (page 37)

1 (a) 2^7 (b) 4^7 (c) 3^4

(d) 5^3 (e) $\dfrac{1}{2^2}$ (f) 7

(g) 2^6 (h) $\frac{1}{3}$ (i) 3^4

2 (a) x^9 (b) x^8 (c) $\dfrac{1}{y^5}$

(d) p^3 (e) q^2 (f) $\dfrac{1}{r^2}$

(g) $\dfrac{1}{t}$ (h) $\dfrac{1}{x^2}$ (i) 1

3 (a) 2^6 (b) 3^{12} (c) 5^8

(d) x^{15} (e) y^6 (f) z^{20}

Exercise 6B (page 38)

1 (a) 2^{18} (b) 3^8 (c) 5^{25}

(d) p^{10} (e) q^{18} (f) r^{12}

(g) $\dfrac{1}{s^{14}}$ (h) $\dfrac{1}{t^{24}}$ (i) $\dfrac{1}{u^{32}}$

(j) $\dfrac{1}{x}$ (k) y^2 (l) z^3

(m) x (n) y^{10} (o) z^{10}

Exercise 6C (page 40)

1 (a) $8p^3q^4$ (b) $45s^4t^2$

(c) $24x^3y^3z^4$ (d) $\dfrac{8a^3}{3b}$

(e) $\dfrac{3}{4mn^3}$ (f) $\frac{2}{3}u^4$

(g) $3a^2b$ (h) $\dfrac{2k^2}{5l}$

(i) $\dfrac{2}{3f}$ (j) $8x^6y^9$

(k) $\dfrac{64p^3}{q^9}$ (l) $\dfrac{9c^2}{d^6}$

2 (a) $\dfrac{4}{xy}$ (b) $\dfrac{2p^2}{5q^7}$

(c) $4b$ (d) $\dfrac{1}{2s^2t^2}$

(e) $\dfrac{3r^3}{8s^5}$ (f) $\dfrac{u^3}{2v}$

(g) $\dfrac{3m^4}{2l^3}$ (h) $\dfrac{2e^5}{3f^2}$

(i) $\frac{4}{27}x^3$ (j) $\dfrac{27p^3q}{8r^6}$

(k) 1 (l) $\dfrac{32ac^4}{b^3}$

3 (a) $7x^2$ (b) $6y^2$ (c) 0

(d) $12z^3$ (e) 0 (f) $10x^4$

(g) $-3a^3$ (h) $-x^6$ (i) $64x^5$

Test exercise 6 (page 41)

1 (a) $2^3 \times 3^3 \times 5^5 = 675\,000$

(b) $\dfrac{2}{3 \times 5} = \dfrac{2}{15}$ (c) $\dfrac{2z}{x^2}$

(d) $\dfrac{12a^2b}{c^3}$ (e) $\dfrac{6r^6t^2}{s^5}$

(f) $\dfrac{n^8}{486lm^3}$

7 Brackets and fractions in equations

Exercise 7A (page 43)

1 (a) $\dfrac{7x+10}{12}$ (b) $\dfrac{12x+1}{6}$

(c) $\dfrac{14x-11}{6}$ (d) $\dfrac{x-2}{12}$

(e) $\frac{4}{3}$ (f) $\dfrac{2x+7}{6}$

(g) $\dfrac{10x-y}{12}$ (h) $\dfrac{-2x+17y}{12}$

(i) 0

2 (a) $\dfrac{13+16x}{12}$ (b) $\dfrac{90-27x}{20}$

(c) $\dfrac{4x-9}{12}$ (d) $\dfrac{17+5x}{6}$

(e) $\dfrac{6-49x}{10}$ (f) $-\frac{2}{3}$

(g) $\dfrac{3x+22}{20}$ (h) $\dfrac{-58x+69y}{28}$

(i) $\dfrac{15-11x}{12}$

Exercise 7B (page 45)

1 (a) $2x$ (b) $8x$ (c) y
   (d) $2p$ (e) $2q+8$ (f) $2a+6$
   (g) $2r-7$ (h) $25t-35$

2 (a) $3x-1$ (b) $4x-1$ (c) x
   (d) $s-6$ (e) -1 (f) -2
   (g) $t-4$ (h) $8t-7$ (i) 0

Exercise 7C (page 48)

1 (a) $\frac{20}{3}$ (b) 6 (c) $\frac{3}{8}$ (d) 5
   (e) 12 (f) $\frac{6}{5}$ (g) $\frac{16}{33}$ (h) $\frac{9}{2}$

2 (a) $\frac{5}{2}$ (b) 3 (c) 1
   (d) 4 (e) -3 (f) 3

3 (a) 4 (b) -2 (c) 3 (d) 4
   (e) 5 (f) -1 (g) 1 (h) 2

Test exercise 7 (page 49)

1 (a) -1 (b) -7 (c) -2
   (d) 1 (e) 0 (f) 9

2 (a) 8 (b) 3 (c) -1
   (d) -2 (e) 0 (f) 4

3 (a) -7 (b) -20 (c) 4
   (d) $\frac{1}{9}$ (e) 7 (f) -1

8 Factorising and brackets

Exercise 8A (page 51)

1 (a) $3(p+3)$ (b) $2(q-3)$
   (c) $2(5r+6)$ (d) $3(s-5)$
   (e) $-2(a-7)$ (f) $-2(2b+3)$
   (g) $-2(4c-3)$ (h) $-3(3d+1)$

2 (a) $8(x+2)$ (b) $9(y+2)$
   (c) $4(z-2)$ (d) $8(t-1)$
   (e) $-4(2x+1)$ (f) $-9(9y-2)$
   (g) $-2(2z+1)$ (h) $-4(4t+1)$

3 (a) $x(x+2)$ (b) $x(2x-1)$
   (c) $-x(1+x)$ (d) $x(x-z)$
   (e) $x(x-3z)$ (f) $-x(x-k)$
   (g) $b(a+x)$ (h) $x(ax+b)$

Exercise 8B (page 52)

1 (a) $ac+ad+bc+bd$
   (b) $pr-ps+qr-qs$
   (c) $ac+ad-bc-bd$
   (d) $pr-ps-qr+qs$
   (e) $ab+ac+2b+2c$
   (f) $x^2-xz-xy+yz$
   (g) $a^2-ac+2ab-2bc$
   (h) $a^2-ab+4a-4b$
   (i) $bc-4c+4b-16$

2 (a) x^2+3x+2 (b) x^2-x-2
   (c) x^2+x-2 (d) x^2-3x+2
   (e) $6x^2+11x+3$ (f) $3x^2+5x+2$
   (g) $6x^2+19x+10$ (h) $2x^2-5x+2$
   (i) $4x^2-25$

3 (a) x^2+2x+1 (b) x^2-2x+1
   (c) x^2-6x+9 (d) $x^2+8x+16$
   (e) $4x^2+4x+1$ (f) $4x^2+12x+9$
   (g) $16x^2-56x+49$ (h) $9x^2-30x+25$
   (i) $4x^2-4x+1$

Exercise 8C (page 54)

1 (a) $(a+1)(x+1)$ (b) $(x+2)(y+2)$
   (c) $(p+4)(q+2)$ (d) $(a+c)(x+y)$
   (e) $(a-2)(b+c)$ (f) $(r-2)(r+s)$
   (g) $(c-3)(c+b)$ (h) $(x-y)(x+3)$
   (i) $(z-a)(z-b)$

2 (a) No factors   (b) $(a+1)(x-1)$
   (c) No factors   (d) $-(a+1)(x+1)$
   (e) No factors   (f) $(r+s)(r-s)$
   (g) No factors   (h) $(q-p)(r-p)$
   (i) $(2p+q)(p-r)$

Test exercise 8 (page 54)

1 (a) $x(a+2)$ (b) $p(q+p)$
   (c) $(q+2)(3+p)$ (d) $(4-t)(z+3)$
   (e) $(2h+3)(h-k)$ (f) $a(x+y-z)$

2 (a) $ac-2a+2c-4$ (b) $2p^2-p-1$
   (c) $x^2-2xz-xy+2yz$ (d) x^2-9y^2
   (e) $y^2-6yz+9z^2$
   (f) $4p^2+12pq+9q^2$

9 Changing the subject of a formula

In this chapter, your answer may take a different form, and still be correct.

Exercise 9A (page 56)

1 (a) $x = b - a$ (b) $x = a - 2b$

(c) $x = a - b$ (d) $x = \frac{1}{2}(b - a)$

(e) $x = \frac{2b}{a}$ (f) $x = \frac{3b}{a}$

(g) $x = \frac{b}{a}$ (h) $x = \frac{2b - c}{a}$

2 (a) $c = y - mx$ (b) $m = \frac{y - c}{x}$

(c) $t = \frac{s}{v}$ (d) $R = \frac{V}{I}$

(e) $s = \frac{v^2 - u^2}{2a}$ (f) $g = \frac{v - u}{t}$

(g) $u = v - gt$ (h) $a = \frac{2s - 2u}{t^2}$

(i) $x = \frac{y - b^2}{a^2}$

Exercise 9B (page 57)

1 (a) $x = \frac{1}{2}(b - 2a)$ (b) $x = 8b - 4a$

(c) $x = 0$ (d) $x = \frac{a}{b + c}$

(e) $x = \frac{a(a + b)}{b}$ (f) $x = \frac{cd - ab}{a}$

(g) $x = \frac{bc}{a}$ (h) $x = \frac{a^2}{b}$

2 (a) $d = vt$ (b) $t = \frac{d}{v}$

(c) $u = \frac{2s - at^2}{2t}$ (d) $a = \frac{2s - 2ut}{t^2}$

(e) $v = u + gt$ (f) $u = v - gt$

(g) $u = \frac{2s - vt}{t}$ (h) $A = a^2 + 4ab$

(i) $x = \frac{y - b^2}{a^2}$

Exercise 9C (page 59)

1 (a) $x = \frac{y}{1 + y}$ (b) $x = \frac{y}{1 - y}$

(c) $x = \frac{y}{y - 1}$ (d) $x = \frac{p}{p - q}$

(e) $x = \frac{u}{r + s - t}$ (f) $x = \frac{c}{a - b}$

(g) $x = \frac{k}{h + k}$ (h) $x = \frac{pq}{p - 2q}$

(i) $x = \frac{ab}{a + b}$ (j) $x = \frac{1}{1 - y}$

(k) $x = \frac{1}{y - 1}$ (l) $x = \frac{y + 1}{y - 1}$

(m) $x = \frac{ab}{a - b}$ (n) $x = \frac{k - 2ky}{y - 1}$

(o) $x = \frac{y - 2}{y - 1}$

2 (a) $T = \frac{100A - 100P}{PR}$

(b) $P = \frac{100A}{100 + RT}$ (c) $a = \frac{2s - dl}{d}$

(d) $d = \frac{2s}{a + l}$ (e) $d = \frac{2s - 2an}{n^2 - n}$

(f) $t = \frac{2s}{u + v}$ (g) $u = \frac{fv}{v - f}$

(h) $m = \frac{2E}{v^2 + 2gh}$

Exercise 9D (page 61)

1 (a) $x = (a - 1)^2$ (b) $x = \pm\sqrt{a^2 + 1}$

(c) $x = \pm\sqrt{a^2 + y^2}$ (d) $x = 0$

(e) $x = (1 + a)^3$ (f) $x = \sqrt[3]{a^3 + 1}$

2 (a) $r = \pm\sqrt{\frac{A}{4\pi}}$ (b) $r = \sqrt[3]{\frac{3V}{4\pi}}$

(c) $x = \sqrt[3]{\frac{a^3b^2 + a^3y^2}{b^2}}$

(d) $y = \pm\sqrt{\frac{x^3}{a}}$

(e) $u = \pm\sqrt{\frac{mv^2 - 2E}{m}}$

(f) $r = \pm\sqrt{\frac{V}{\pi h}}$

Test exercise 9 (page 62)

1 (a) $x = \dfrac{c}{2b}$ (b) $x = \dfrac{2s - ny}{n}$

(c) $x = 0$ (d) $x = \dfrac{a + b}{b + c}$

(e) $x = \dfrac{ay}{y - b}$ (f) $x = \sqrt[3]{\dfrac{a^3 b^3 - a^3 y^3}{b^3}}$

2 (a) $r = \dfrac{s - a}{s}$ (b) $h = \dfrac{A - 2\pi r^2}{2\pi r}$

(c) $f = \dfrac{uv}{u + v}$ (d) $t = \pm\sqrt{\dfrac{2h}{g}}$

(e) $x = \pm\sqrt{\dfrac{w^2 a^2 - v^2}{w^2}}$

(f) $s = \sqrt[3]{72\pi V^2}$

10 Factorising quadratics

Exercise 10A (page 63)

1 (a) $a = 1, b = 3, c = 5$
(b) $a = 1, b = -1, c = 7$
(c) $a = 3, b = 2, c = -1$
(d) $a = 1, b = 0, c = -4$
(e) $a = 5, b = 0, c = 1$
(f) $a = -1, b = -2, c = 4$

2 (a) $x^2 - 3x + 2$ (b) $2x^2 - 5$
(c) $-3x^2 - x + 4$ (d) $x^2 - 3x$

Exercise 10B (page 66)

1 (a) $(x + 1)(x + 2)$ (b) $(x + 1)(x + 3)$
(c) $(x + 2)^2$ (d) $(y + 1)(y + 8)$
(e) $(x + 2)(x + 5)$ (f) $(x + 3)^2$
(g) $(x + 3)(x + 8)$ (h) $(p + 4)(p + 5)$
(i) $(x + 3)(x + 6)$ (j) $(k + 1)(k + 21)$
(k) $(x + 5)(x + 6)$ (l) $(x + 4)(x + 15)$

2 (a) $(x - 1)(x - 3)$ (b) $(a - 1)(a - 4)$
(c) $(x - 1)(x - 6)$ (d) $(x - 1)(x - 8)$
(e) $(x - 1)^2$ (f) $(l - 3)(l - 4)$
(g) $(z - 2)(z - 11)$ (h) $(x - 5)^2$
(i) $(x - 4)(x - 7)$ (j) $(x - 4)(x - 8)$
(k) $(q - 5)(q - 7)$ (l) $(x - 6)(x - 10)$

3 (a) $(x - 1)(x + 2)$ (b) $(x - 2)(x + 1)$
(c) $(c - 4)(c + 1)$ (d) $(x - 2)(x + 3)$

(e) $(d - 4)(d + 2)$ (f) $(x - 1)(x + 8)$
(g) $(h - 2)(h + 11)$ (h) $(x - 4)(x + 3)$
(i) $(x - 3)(x + 8)$ (j) $(x - 6)(x + 3)$
(k) $(x - 4)(x + 14)$ (l) $(n - 12)(n + 5)$

4 (a) $(s - 4)(s + 1)$ (b) $(x - 5)(x - 8)$
(c) No factors (d) $(x - 5)(x + 2)$
(e) No factors (f) $(t + 3)(t + 5)$
(g) $(x - 9)(x + 1)$ (h) No factors
(i) $(x + 1)(x - 9)$ (j) $(x + 2)(x + 7)$
(k) No factors (l) $(y + 5)^2$
(m) No factors (n) $(x - 3)(x + 7)$
(o) $(x - 3)(x - 11)$ (p) No factors
(q) $(j - 10)(j + 6)$ (r) $(x - 4)(x + 15)$
(s) No factors (t) $(x - 2)(x + 2)$
(u) $x \times x$

Exercise 10C (page 68)

1 (a) $(x + 1)(2x + 1)$ (b) $(x - 2)(2x - 1)$
(c) $(x + 1)(3x + 2)$ (d) $(x - 1)(2x - 5)$
(e) $(x - 2)(3x - 2)$ (f) $(2x + 1)(3x + 1)$
(g) $(3x - 1)^2$ (h) $(3x + 2)^2$
(i) $(2x - 1)(2x - 5)$ (j) $(2x - 3)(3x - 2)$
(k) $(3x + 2)(x + 4)$ (l) $(4x + 1)(15x + 1)$

2 (a) $(2x + 1)(x - 1)$ (b) $(3x - 1)(x + 1)$
(c) $(3x + 1)(2x - 1)$ (d) $(4x - 1)(3x + 1)$
(e) $(2x - 1)(x + 2)$ (f) $(2x - 3)(x + 1)$
(g) $(4x + 1)(x - 2)$ (h) $(3x + 2)(x - 2)$
(i) $(8x + 1)(x - 2)$ (j) $(2x + 3)(3x - 2)$
(k) $(2x - 5)(2x + 1)$ (l) $(3x + 2)(2x - 5)$

3 (a) $2(x - 1)(x + 2)$ (b) $4(x + 2)^2$
(c) $3(3x - 1)(x - 3)$ (d) $4(x - 1)(x + 3)$
(e) $6(x + 3)^2$ (f) $2(2x - 5)(2x - 1)$
(g) $2(3x - 4)(2x + 1)$
(h) $2(2x + 5)(x + 1)$ (i) $2(3x + 2)^2$

4 (a) $(2 + x)(1 + x)$ (b) $(2 - x)(1 + 2x)$
(c) $(4 - x)(1 + x)$ (d) $(6 + x)(1 - x)$
(e) $(5 - x)(2 + x)$ (f) $(2 + 3x)(1 - x)$
(g) $(4 - 3x)(1 + 2x)$ (h) $(4 + 5x)(2 - 3x)$
(i) $(2 + 3x)(3 - 4x)$

Exercise 10D (page 70)

1 (a) $(x + 1)(x - 1)$ (b) $(x + 9)(x - 9)$
(c) $(2x + 3)(2x - 3)$ (d) $(3x + 1)(3x - 1)$
(e) $(2 + 5d)(2 - 5d)$ (f) $8(z + 2)(z - 2)$

2   (a) $3(x+3)(x-3)$ (b) $2(5+y)(5-y)$

    (c) $4(5+z)(5-z)$ (d) $(1-x)(1+3x)$

    (e) $(x+1)(3x+1)$ (f) $(x+4)(3x-2)$

Test exercise 10 (page 71)

1   (a) $x(3x+2)$ (b) $(1+x)(1+3x)$

    (c) $(3+5y)(3-5y)$ (d) $(3p-2)(p+2)$

    (e) $3(x-1)(x-4)$ (f) $6(s^2+9)$

    (g) $x(4-5x)$ (h) $(2a-5)^2$

    (i) $2(1+w)(1-w)$ (j) $(4x+3)(3x-2)$

    (k)   No factors   (l) $2(2t-1)(2t+5)$

    (m) $3(2-3x)^2$ (n) $2(1+2x^2)$

    (o) $2(7-x)(3+x)$

11 Quadratic equations

Exercise 11A (page 74)

1   (a) $x^2+2x-5=0$

    (b) $2x^2-x-10=0$

    (c) $x^2-4x-3=0$

    (d) $x^2-4x-3=0$

    (e) $3x^2-2x-1=0$

    (f) $7x^2-9x-5=0$

2   (a) $-1,-2$ (b) $1,3$ (c) 2

    (d) $-1,4$ (e) $-4,-5$ (f) $5,7$

    (g) $-5,3$ (h) $-5,-6$ (i) $-14,4$

    (j) $4,8$ (k) -5 (l) $-3,4$

3   (a) $-3,0$ (b) $0,4$ (c) $-2,2$

    (d) $-5,5$ (e) $-\frac{25}{4},0$ (f) $-\frac{5}{2},\frac{5}{2}$

4   (a) $-\frac{1}{2},1$ (b) $-\frac{2}{3},\frac{3}{4}$ (c) $-\frac{1}{2},\frac{4}{3}$

    (d) $-\frac{1}{4},2$ (e) $-\frac{2}{3},\frac{5}{2}$ (f) $\frac{1}{2},\frac{5}{2}$

Exercise 11B (page 77)

1   (a) $-2,-5$ (b) $4,5$ (c) $-3,6$

    (d) $1,\frac{5}{2}$ (e) $-2,\frac{2}{3}$ (f) $-\frac{1}{2},\frac{3}{2}$

    (g) $\frac{4}{3}$ (h) $-3,9$ (i) $-\frac{16}{3},1$

2   (a) $-5.30,-1.70$ (b) $1.15, 7.85$

    (c) $-1.19, 4.19$ (d) $-0.550, 4.55$

    (e) $-2.23, 0.897$ (f) $-1.23, 1.90$

    (g) $-0.836, 1.44$ (h) $-0.699, 1.07$

    (i) $-1.20, 1.45$

3   (a) $-1.45, 3.45$ (b) $-1.12, 3.12$

    (c)   No roots   (d) $\frac{1}{3},6$

    (e)   No roots   (f) $-100, 0.0999$

    (g) $0.785, 2.55$ (h) $-0.382, 2.62$

    (i)   No roots

Test exercise 11 (page 78)

1   (a) $\frac{1}{2},3$ (b) $-\frac{1}{2},4$

    (c) $-1.12, 3.12$ (d)   No roots

    (e) $-\frac{3}{4},2$ (f) $-1.62, 0.618$

12 Simultaneous equations

Exercise 12A (page 80)

1   (a) $6x=12$ (b) $2x=8$

    (c) $-5x=10$ (d) $5y=10$

    (e) $-7y=14$ (f) $-y=6$

2   (a) $x=2$ (b) $8x=0$

    (c) $2x=-2$ (d) $y=6$

    (e) $y=-4$ (f) $7y=21$

Exercise 12B (page 82)

1   (a) $x=2, y=1$ (b) $x=4, y=16$

    (c) $x=-2, y=3$ (d) $x=-\frac{1}{3}, y=2$

    (e) $x=-1, y=-2$ (f) $x=33, y=-6$

2   (a) $x=2, y=1$ (b) $x=0, y=-4$

    (c) $x=-1, y=-1$ (d) $x=-9, y=6$

    (e) $x=7, y=-4$ (f) $x=-3, y=3$

Exercise 12C (page 85)

1   (a) $x=\frac{19}{5}, y=-\frac{3}{5}$ (b) $x=-1, y=3$

    (c) $x=-2, y=3$ (d) $x=\frac{1}{2}, y=-1$

    (e) $x=\frac{11}{2}, y=3$ (f) $x=7, y=2$

    (g) $x=2, y=3$ (h) $x=4, y=2$

    (i) $x=1, y=-3$

2   (a) $x=2, y=2$ (b) $x=2, y=1$

    (c) $x=4, y=-1$ (d) $x=0.3, y=0.2$

    (e) $x=-0.1, y=0.6$ (f) $x=0.5, y=0.25$

    (g) $x=\frac{1}{3}, y=-\frac{2}{3}$ (h) $x=-\frac{3}{4}, y=\frac{1}{8}$

    (i) $x=0.7, y=-0.6$

Test exercise 12 (page 85)

1   (a) $x=\frac{21}{2}, y=\frac{5}{2}$ (b) $x=-19, y=18$

    (c) $x=-4, y=-3$ (d) $x=3, y=0$

    (e) $x=1, y=-1$ (f) $x=20, y=10$

13 Trigonometry

Exercise 13A (page 89)

1 (a) p, r, q (b) m, l, n (c) y, x, z
   (d) b, c, a (e) t, r, s (f) f, d, e

2 (a) 30°   (b) 63.6°
   (c) 51.3°   (d) 12.1 cm
   (e) 11.3 cm (f) 3.5 cm

3 (a) 14.1 cm (b) 34.8°
   (c) 31.1 cm (d) 33.7°
   (e) 10.4 cm (f) 5.20 cm

4 (a) 17.9 cm (b) 15.5 cm
   (c) 9.33 cm (d) 13.9 cm
   (e) 35.1 cm (f) 10.9 cm

Exercise 13B (page 90)

1 (a) 0.342, 0.342   (b) 0.5, 0.5
   (c) 0.574, 0.574   (d) 0.515, 0.515
   (e) 0.682, 0.682   (f) 0.035, 0.035
   $\sin\theta° = \sin(180 - \theta)°$

2 (a) 0.940, −0.940 (b) 0.866, −0.866
   (c) 0.819, −0.819 (d) 0.857, −0.857
   (e) 0.731, −0.731 (f) 0.999, −0.999
   $\cos\theta° = -\cos(180 - \theta)°$

Exercise 13C (page 92)

1 (a) 150   (b) 162.5   (c) 120

2 (a) 150   (b) 161.9   (c) 45

3 (a) 107.5 (b) 7.1, 172.9
   (c) 72.5   (d) 8.6, 171.4
   (e) 90   (f) 90

Test exercise 13 (page 93)

1 (a) 7.19 cm, 1.27 cm
   (b) 6.22 cm, 43.7°

2 (a) 66.4   (b) 113.6
   (c) 23.6, 156.4 (d) 0, 180
   (e) 53.1, 126.9 (f) 45, 135

14 The sine rule for a triangle

Exercise 14A (page 98)

1 (a) 78 cm^2 (b) 18.4 cm^2
   (c) 6 cm^2 (d) 10.5 cm^2
   (e) 0.0698 cm^2 (f) 13.9 cm^2

2 (a) 9.05 cm^2 (b) 4.53 cm^2

3 (a) 32.2°, 147.8°   (b) 15.5°, 164.5°
   (c) 81.0°, 99.0°   (d) Not possible
   (e) 30°, 150°   (f) 27.9°, 152.1°

Exercise 14B (page 101)

1 (a) 4.48 cm   (b) 9.45 cm
   (c) 5.89 cm   (d) 7.06 cm
   (e) 7.67 cm   (f) 8.35 cm

2 (a) 58.5°, 121.5°   (b) 80.5°, 99.5°
   (c) 30.0°   (d) 33.5°, 146.5°
   (e) 53.1°   (f) 49.6°, 130.4°

Test exercise 14 (page 102)

1 (a) 291 cm^2 (b) 58.4 cm^2

2 (a) 5.36 cm, 13.3 cm
   (b) 37.2 cm, 48.4 cm

3 (a) $Y = 60.9°$, $Z = 37.1°$
   (b) $A = 13.8°$, $B = 156.2°$ or
        $A = 166.2°$, $B = 3.8°$

15 The cosine rule for a triangle

Exercise 15A (page 107)

1 (a) 14.3 cm   (b) 14.9 cm
   (c) 5 cm   (d) 12.6 cm
   (e) 0.070 cm   (f) 6.93 cm

2 (a) 104.5°   (b) 78.5°
   (c) 117.3°   (d) 21.6°
   (e) 120.4°
   (f) The value of $\cos F$ is −2.9, which is
        impossible.

3 (a) 57.0°, 80.2° (b) 76.4°, 49.5°
   (c) 90°, 36.9°   (d) 31.5°, 41.3°
   (e) 48.3°, 70.2° (f) 36.2°, 64.1°

Test exercise 15 (page 107)

1 (a) 5.12 cm   (b) 25.3 cm

2 (a) 83.8°, 40.7°, 55.4°
   (b) 141.1°, 19.7°, 19.3°

Index

Printed in the United States
By Bookmasters